Son of Old Jules

SON OF OLD JULES

Memoirs of Jules Sandoz, Jr.

by

Caroline Sandoz Pifer

and

Jules Sandoz, Jr.

University of Nebraska Press
Lincoln and London

The paper in this publication meets the minimum requirements of
American National Standard for Information Sciences—
Permanence of Paper for Printed Library Materials, ANSI Z39.48–
1984.

First Bison Book printing: 1989
Most recent printing indicated by the first digit below:
1 2 3 4 5 6 7 8 9 10

Library of Congress Cataloging-in-Publication Data

Pifer, Caroline Sandoz.
Son of Old Jules: memoirs of Jules Sandoz, Jr. / by Caroline
Sandoz Pifer and Jules Sandoz, Jr.
p.   cm.
Reprint. Originally published: 1st ed. Crawford, NE: Cottonwood
Press, © 1987.
ISBN 0-8032-4199-2.   ISBN 0-8032-9190-6 (pbk.)
  1. Sandoz, Jules, 1897–1980.   2. Sandoz, Jules Ami, 1857?–1928.
3. Pioneers—Nebraska—Biography.   4. Frontier and pioneer
life—Nebraska.   5. Nebraska—Biography.   6. Sandhills
(Neb.)—Social life and customs.   I. Sandoz, Jules, 1897–1980.
II. Title.
F666.S347P54   1989   88-19138
978.2'02'0924—dc19   CIP

Reprinted by arrangement with Caroline Sandoz Pifer

Previously copyrighted material used by permission of the *Omaha*
(Nebraska) *World-Herald:* "Memoirs of Jules Sandoz, Jr." series—
November 12, 1978 (Chapter I), October 21, 1979 (Chapter II),
January 22, 1984 (Chapter III), August 5, 1984 (Chapter IV), January
13, 1985 (Chapter V), February 2, 1986 (Chapter VI).

Contents

Photographs
(between pages 62 and 63)

Jules Alexander Sandoz, Jr.
Mary Fehr Sandoz and Sandoz Children (1901)
The Riverplace on the Niobrara (about 1910)
Caroline Sandoz Pifer and Jules Sandoz, Jr. (1978)

Introduction

This book is meant to supplement, not contradict, the book *Old Jules* written by our sister Mari Sandoz and published in 1935. In 1978 my brother, the Jules Alexander Sandoz, Jr., of the story, became ill with cancer and had to sell his ranch. My husband, Robert Pifer, had died, and my two daughters, Eleanor and Mary Ann, were grown and lived elsewhere. So Jules came to live with me. He was tense and nervous, and to fill the time, he started telling the story of his life to me and my hired man, George Crawford. My brother seemed to approve of our sister telling the story of our family, and with encouragement, he decided he wanted his story told, to give a more balanced view of the settler period.

Since there was no one else interested, we made an agreement that I would write it and share any profits with his two daughters, Celia Ostrander and Marguerite Widfeldt. We tried to tape record to give us definite information, but his voice was too far gone. At one time, he sat down in his room and managed to write seventy-five pages in longhand. This became an important piece in my work, for while it was quite clear he could not write a complete story, because there was too much repetition, lack of coherence, and little knowledge of the mechanics of writing, it gave me valuable clues to his style and vocabulary.

My hired man was a good listener and willing to make his own coffee, so it left me free to take down notes on Jules' experiences. Since a notebook was intimidating, I used the backs of old envelopes, scratch paper, dated calendars, whatever. Nor could I interrupt for verification of facts or additions; anything at all made him lose his flow of thought and recede within himself.

But he had only told the story as far as his marriage when the cancer of the bone became worse, and he went to live with his daughter Celia for a time. From there he went to the St. Joseph Gerontology Center in Alliance, Nebraska. He died February 5, 1980, eighty-two years after his birth December 27, 1897, on the Niobrara Riverplace at Grayson, Nebraska, the second child, first son of Jules Ami Sandoz and Mary Fehr Sandoz. If any of his family wishes to write about him further, there is ample material, for in later years he became more than a millionaire and famous for his eccentricities.

The first of these chapters appeared, written in the first person, in the *Omaha* (Nebraska) *World-Herald* Midlands section in 1978, so he was able to read it in print. I had been writing for the paper for some time about Mari and our life on the early homestead, so it was easy for me to change over to his stories. We used the name Mari for our

writing sister because that had become her legal name.
Jules originally called our father "Dada," but eventually changed to "Papa," as all the rest of us called him.

After Jules was gone, I had to come to terms with immersing myself in his story to the extent that I could carry on the rest of the book in the first person. While he could not write much more than a letter, he expressed himself well in conversation. He used an inordinate amount of big words along with considerable German sentence structure. He was largely self-educated and came up with some unusual word pronunciations. The bigger words made it easier for me, as I was working on a degree in literature at the time. He was the only man I ever knew who subscribed to the *Congressional Record* and actually read it word for word. We bought one of his places at one time, and there were stacks of those finely-printed thin-paper publications dog-eared from use.

Many of Jules' stories were repetitious, but I took them all down to compare and evaluate. Clearly some of his memories were faulty. Time and circumstances made them impossible. So I balanced his tales with what Mari had in her book, with maps, and old newspaper accounts, as with the snakebite story. When I could, I used both accounts, but if it was a question of Jules' memory against another, I took his.

By typing all of his notes in separate paragraphs, I could cut them apart and arrange them on fresh sheets of paper with glue. By observing sequences of time and place, then deleting repetitions, I could type them off, cut them again, and rearrange for dramatic value and human interest. In this way, I went through five revisions. I hope now I have made a readable addition not only to the

x   history of our family, but to the history of our area, and at the same time made a tribute to a beloved brother who, while thirteen years my senior, and surely of a different time and place in our family, still was a vital influence in my upbringing. He made the past eight years of this writing a stimulating and significant part of my life.

Caroline Sandoz Pifer

Son of Old Jules

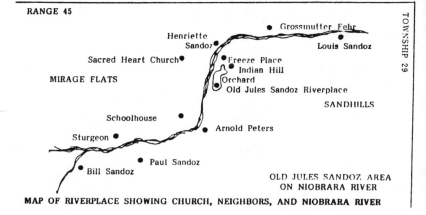

MAP OF RIVERPLACE SHOWING CHURCH, NEIGHBORS, AND NIOBRARA RIVER

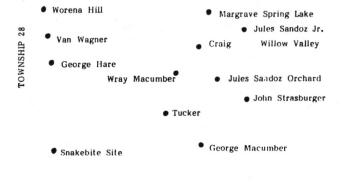

HOMESTEAD LOCALITY IN SANDHILLS, SHERIDAN COUNTY, NEBRASKA

Chapter I

Grossmutter

I grew up in a woman's world until I was six. No one thought I would live, so small, so blue, and so puny when born, the second child of Old Jules and Mary Sandoz. My grandmother Fehr, called "Grossmutter" in the German language of my family, was free to take me upstairs in our Riverplace house where she slept and cared for me.

Grossmutter was a small, roundish woman with dark hair pulled back into a bun, her prominent nose probably a throwback to the Romans who once held the Rhine River in her homeland in Switzerland. I was seldom downstairs until I was able to join this Swiss-German in her work. But even when I was with the family, I was always with Mama, my sister Mari (a year older), or Mama's sister Susie, always females. Papa scarcely noticed me. It was Mari he favored, when he favored anyone.

My grandmother took me along to her work, which seemed continual: chopping wood in winter, picking fruit, hoeing and pulling weeds in summer. She could even pull poison ivy barehanded. "Verdampt Unkraut" she called it. This little foreigner then was my whole world, and I scarcely considered myself part of the family. Anyway, while Mari was just eighteen months older, she was usually lost in a world of fantasy and make-believe.

My first recollections are of a wonderful upstairs filled with the pungent smell of drying onions and garlic, dried green beans strung on coarse thread hanging from nails in the rafters, cloth sacks of dried corn, currants, chokecherries and plums with sheets of paper, bark, anything flat, covered with more drying edibles on the floor by the tall west window and by the warm chimney. I liked that window from which I could look at the fine sweep of the Niobrara River up towards Mirage Flats and the Catholic church. In winter, at night, the full moon shone on the ice. It was my lookout to see Mari, as soon as she could walk well, following Papa on his daily hunt.

Our bed was of the usual feather tick filled with down from the ducks and geese that Papa shot. We slept on a mattress of cottonwood leaves. Since Grossmutter did not condone nudity, I slept in my underwear and really did not know what my body looked like, much less hers, which was always well-covered. In fact I grew up considering even bare feet suspect and howled if I had to go without shoes.

However, my religious training was not neglected. I was baptized along with James and Mari into the Immanuel Lutheran church that met every two weeks in our home with Pastor Haeckel. My grandmother read to me every day from her German Bible. This book had no New Testament, so I am illiterate in the teachings of Christ. And since Papa believed only in the Jewish Ten Commandments, the cajolings of my Christian friends are apt to fall on unknowing ears.

Then when I was about five, my grandmother got a small scratch of a plum thorn above one eye. It did not heal and soon emerged as a dark sore. Papa wanted her to go to Omaha to a surgeon and have it removed. "Ach, I will not then have myself butchered," she said in her German-Swiss.

Consequently, the lesion enlarged, and soon began the sharp continuing pain, the swelling and the misery. She could no longer help me up and down the stairs, nor climb them herself. Now she had her bed in the lean-to, the one built for the exquisite Rosalie, Papa's former sweetheart in Switzerland who did not choose to live in wild America. I was put to sleeping with Mari downstairs. Henry Teagle recalled in a letter to Mari in 1941 that he shared our bed during a stop at our house at the turn of the century.

During the years that Grossmutter struggled with cancer, my world fell apart. I had not been taught to mind, and got whipping after whipping. When I filled the seed potato bucket with sand, Papa thrashed me until he was played out, but I did not give in. Then they tried to rule me by ridicule. In fact, one time I bit Mari on the arm on a birthmark she had; they called me "Menchenfresser," German for "maneater." I have been disciplined throughout my life for my nonconformity.

4   I often longed to go to my ailing grandparent, but she would have big bandages over her face, praying endlessly that God might take her from such affliction. Finally I found a new friend and crony in my brother, James, eighteen months younger than I. We became a duet that rebelled against the bossiness of Mari. We went hunting and trapping together and with Papa, and I learned from James the fun of swimming naked.

It was on one of these hunting trips that James and I were dogging quail for Papa and a friend. It was close to where we had some traps set for rock rabbits, which were thick along the limestone banks. I raised up briefly to go and look at the setting when there was a blast and I fell back, shot in the head. Fortunately, it was only birdshot, and Papa took me home and dug out the pellets, except two—one in each ear—that I've carried all my life.

When Grandmother died, we were taken in a wagon some three miles to the Swiss graveyard to the southeast. All the way I cried because they were putting her in the ground and the badgers would dig her up. I could do nothing about it. Many years later, I visited the grave, and as I had suspected, the badgers had dug mightily, but apparently never penetrated the pine box laid north and south. So my good grandparent rests at peace with herself and, I suppose, "Herr Gott."

Chapter II

The Winter Papa Was in Jail

When Grossmutter Fehr died, Papa was made administrator and divided her property as he saw fit. She had proved up on 160 acres on Spring Creek just north of our place on the Niobrara River and across from it. He had built a small house for her, and she had lived there enough to prove residency. She had bought a cow, our only milk cow for several years, and figured in ten years to have fifty head of cattle. In seven years she did have twenty-five head and probably would have made her count had she lived. Papa gave Uncle Jake and Aunt Susie the cattle and kept the land, which gave us some much-needed pasture. Aunt Susie's husband, Uncle Charlie Grossenbacher, did not agree with this division and said so loudly, causing a rift between Aunt Susie and us as long as Papa lived.

This must have caused Mama much sorrow because she and Aunt Susie were very close, talked daily on the telephone. Then for twenty-five years, they no longer saw or called each other.

I had been living upstairs with Grossmutter, and, after she died, I had to join a family I felt alien to, and, in addition, about that time we got a new baby brother, Fritz, a demanding baby. Because of a rupture at birth, he could not be allowed to cry. With no discipline, he soon went rampant through everything. His howling was enough to bring even father to terms. If he saw Papa take rice at the breakfast table, he demanded the rest in the bowl. When Mama said the rest of us should have some, he howled and Papa shoved him the bowl. "Give it to him, give it to him." When Uncle Paul Sandoz came to visit after his wife (the former Fanny Ponchon) died, he brought us big boxes of fine toys—tennis sets, marbles, a Jack-in-the-Box—as he was on his way back to Switzerland. Fritz broke and lost them, those he didn't chew to pieces. Later the Surbers gave us a fine autoharp of excellent tone, one their wealthy Jewish friends the Goulds had given them. Long before anyone could learn to play, Fritz pulled all the strings loose and broke the sounding board.

Meanwhile, Papa had gotten into trouble with the neighbors upriver. There was a corporation of two brothers-in-law, one a sharp man of the Peters family, the other a loyal follower. They had both married daughters of the Texas Moravian named Jahn. Their families were basically good people. The mother of the wives was my godmother. Yet the quarrel developed, especially after the lax brother-in-law, Kollers, got some wolfhounds while Papa was running two or three dozen unbroken horses on the range where the corporation wanted to run their cattle. There was friction over this government land that lay directly above and east of our house on a flat.

One summer evening, Papa went out as he usually did to listen for any activity around and to contemplate the next day's weather. I went out with him, as did a German immigrant who was in the area looking for free land. We heard horses running, dogs barking, barb wire creaking and posts snapping off. We knew at once it was the neighbor's wolfhounds running our horses in the school section—the free land. Grabbing a rifle from over the door, Papa aimed it at the sky and shot several times. It was already too dark to see much and the pasture lay over the hill, but the noise of the shooting would surely scare off the dogs. I was standing just behind him, watching the rifle barrel in the air to see the burning powder follow the shots. Those two neighbors hauled him into court for shooting at them.

The lawyer for the prosecution called the German as witness. This would-be settler did not speak English and gave the distance to the pasture in kilometers. As the interpreter did not understand the metric system, he translated it as three miles. That would have been a lie, so the judge threw out the testimony, and our parent was declared guilty. The fine was for one hundred dollars or thirty days in jail. Papa elected to sit it out, as my sister Mari wrote of the Kollers-Peters shooting in her book *Old Jules*.

The winter turned bad; the snow got deep. Four-wire fences were buried. We kids sat on top of the pitch pine posts sticking out of the snow, no wire in sight. We didn't have much to eat. There was considerable sentiment in the community against those who had deprived us of someone to furnish game and furs for ur livelihood. Different neighbors offered to pay the fine, including Uncle Bill. Mama said it would only encourage the county attorney to bring other lawsuits, and so Papa indignantly refused. The neighbors then suggested that we get money from the county for groceries since they had our parent in jail and could legally be made to support the family. But Mama was far too proud to accept charity, and so we made out the best we could.

James and I increased our traplines. We were trapping three miles of river, a mile and a half each way, catching rock rabbits for our daily meat and catching muskrats for their furs. We earned a hundred and fifty dollars that winter. We had dried fruits that escaped the hail, but with Fritz a baby and Mari too spindly and little to cut wood, James and I had the added chore of getting fuel to burn, while Mama cut turnips to feed the cattle. We ran a bucksaw, holding it at the opposite end. I never had another partner that was half as good as James, so cutting the wood was not such a problem, but first finding it, and then hauling it home, was.

I worried every night until I went to sleep trying to think how and where James and I could find enough sticks of wood for the next day. We never had any fuel ahead now that Papa was in jail, and we were surviving only from day to day. We had cut all the brush as far downriver as the Freese Hanging Tree. There were a few

uncut plum bushes beyond that point, but it was a long
way to bring it home on our homemade sled.

Mama bundled us up in hand-knitted caps, mittens, and scarves, and we were warm enough going and while sawing and breaking the smaller branches over our knees, but when we started home, the cold began to penetrate. One bitter day, the ice was reaching far out over the Niobrara River, now only a ten-foot open channel, with the current back and forth on each side underneath. It created a hazard for unsuspecting cattle and, yes, humans who would be careless and overly-brave. We didn't think we really needed the frequent warnings of our parents about falling through, for I was scared of the river, the water, and practically everything else anyway. But we had run our traplines and sawed and broken a load of wood for the rickety box on our sled and were terribly tired and awfully cold. We decided to pull the load the half-mile upstream on the ice by the bank, where it was usually quite thick, even if it was risky. I was ahead pulling on the sled rope, testing the ice with a blunt stick, and James was behind pushing. We were just below the Hanging Tree where the river current is particularly un-certain, when suddenly I felt the sled giving way behind me. I looked back to see James disappearing into the river.

Quickly I pulled the rope from the sled and ran back on the bank to the hole, but could see nothing except the churning ice chunks. I knew James was drowning, but there was no way to help. I thought, how could I tell Mama that James was gone. Everything was bad anyway—the hail of the past summer, the trial, Papa in jail. I howled, "James! James!" because there was nothing else to do. But James was an especially strong swimmer, and better-sized for his age than I. It was as if he were coming back from the dead to see his soggy knitted cap push up among the ice pieces, then his mittened hands grab for something solid. I threw him the rope, and working together, he came up out of the icy water. It was a cold trip as we ran all the way to the house, where Mama quickly changed James' frozen clothes and wrapped him in a blanket before the oven.

Later, Mama and I went back down the river and brought the wood home up through the orchard, thankful our James was safe.

Chapter III

School in the Peters District

Early in the 1900s while Papa was in the Sheridan County jail in Rushville for allegedly shooting at Frank Koller and Arnold Peters, he wrote to President Theodore Roosevelt about the rancher and settler problems. His thirty-day sentence passed, and he was freed, but he did not come home. Instead, he went to the land office in Alliance to contest all of what he called fraudulent filings in the pasture of Koller and of Arnold Peters. When these two men could not get the hoboes who had made out the papers to defend their homesteads, Peters, being a shrewd man, came to a settlement with our father. We bought a piece of trust land in their pasture, and they gave us an indefinite lease on the 160 acres connected with our homeplace on the east. Papa then withdrew all the contests on the filings.

We had been running the Grayson post office, but as a result of going to jail, Papa lost it, and Grayson was moved five miles down the Niobrara to the Keplinger place. Now, in going after the mail the first time, Mari and I followed most of the way along an old Mormon trail made by Conestoga wagons with their wider-than-standard tracks. The Keplingers had dogs, and one had even bitten our father. We had no dog, so I was afraid, although I guess my sister was not. She had a way with dogs. It was five miles there and five miles back, but I did not mind the walk, only the dogs. Eventually, John Peters got a mail route established a mile west of our home past the original Sandoz homestead on Mirage Flats and a post office further on in the Peters name. So we put up a mailbox and ended the dog worries.

Before losing the post office, we had been making part of our living with truck gardening. A half-acre of asparagus had been planted some years back, and in season it was cut and gathered into pound bunches and sent to Rushville with the mail carrier and sold in Asay's store. This wholesale gardening was akin to Papa's role in life as he saw it. He wanted to feed people. One year he planted rows of peas the entire length of the orchard, about a half mile long. These were between the rows of trees, and besides furnishing produce, they could prevent the soil from blowing away from the tree roots.

That Fourth of July, when James and I were about eight and nine years old, we were to pull a garden cultivator called in German a "Garta Machina," which loosely means a "garden machine." It was equipped with a three-inch plow, or a seeder, or cultivator shovels. A rope was knotted to a pull hook with a stick across the outer end, and one boy on each side put it against his chest and

pulled. Papa started us out plowing by holding the handles on the first round, and then, on the second round,
Mari was to do the guiding and hang on the best she
could. We estimated that it was going to be a nine-mile
pull if and when we ever finished those peas. Buggies and
wagons rumbled across the bridge from the Mirage Flats
west and up the road just east of our house on their way to
a celebration down the Niobrara River at Palmer's grove.
When the young Heesackers went by, they stood up in
their wagon and called loudly for us to come along. This
was too much, and we jerked the machine out of Mari's
hands and staged a runaway. We ran all the way down to
the river, broke off both handles and lost the plow in the
water. Mari went to the house to sit on one of the sawed-
off gateposts to watch the traffic. By the time Papa found
out about it, the incident was old, the plow was recovered, and only some occasional swearing accompanied
the replacing of the handles.

After losing the mail service to our house, Papa tried
selling garden produce at various places. One time he was
taking a load across to sell in Alliance, and included was a
flour sack full of shelled peas from those long rows. The
team ran away, as they so often did, and spilled the green
peas for a mile across Mirage Flats. Papa never could get
himself to wind the lines on the wheel hub on stopping.
One of the horses struck out over the neck yoke and broke
its leg. It had to be shot, and he limped home leading the
other horse. So now we had no team.

The next spring he hired forty acres of the land acquired from Peters plowed for corn. We raised a fine crop,
not doing any cultivating because we could not afford it.
Instead, the family would go up there, Mama carrying

Fritz, who was the baby, in a box on her head, balancing it with one hand and carrying a hoe in the other. We hoed the corn three times, James and Mama and I, sometimes with Papa and Tom Welsch helping. Mari took care of Fritz at one end of the field. In the fall when the corn was ripe, they hitched James and me to a two-wheeled cart with an eight-foot lightweight tongue to pull by. We pulled with our chests against a stick, just as we had done on the "Garta Machina," or just as a horse would do in the collar. When we got to a washout at one side of the field, Mama and Welsch would get behind and push. We unloaded at the end of the field where Mari was.

Later that fall, Papa got Tom Taylor to break a three-year-old colt out of his old saddle mare Daisy, and we hauled the corn home.

Now when he wanted a team to drive, they were in a pasture a mile from home, dragging fifty-foot ropes. We'd get hold of the ropes, and they'd stop to wait. Upon coiling the ropes to the horses' heads, we'd apply a half-hitch around their noses and climb on to ride home. That was the extent of our riding, however, only to bring the team home. We never went anyplace on horseback, always on foot.

During the legal wrangling over the shooting, the courts discovered Papa had two children of school age not attending anywhere. The county superintendent notified him that we must be sent to school at once. The schoolhouse in our district was about five miles east in the Sandhills, so it was decided we would attend the Peters school a mile and a half southwest across the Minten pasture on the Flats. This was a school attended by most of the Peters clan, of whom there were four families with from nine to thirteen children each. They were American Hollanders from Green Bay, Wisconsin, and of the fifty-five children in the sod schoolhouse, most were from these families. The first teacher we had was one of the fathers, George Peters, and he was a good one.

But we were unwelcome outsiders in this school. In the first place, we did not speak English. As long as Grossmutter lived with us, our language was German. So we were made fun of for our talk. And our clothes were not of the American fashion. Also, we were Protestants, although after Grossmutter died and the Weigel family moved away, we quit having Lutheran church in our home, and Fritz was not even baptized. But we were not Catholics, nor were we full-fledged Americans, or so it seemed.

To me, though, the language barrier was the worst. I could not learn the American way of saying, for instance, "twenty-four." In German it is four and twenty, and although I knew the multiplication tables to the twenty-fives, I knew nothing of them in English. And the phonics threw me as I had learned the Latin vowels—and with the German umlaut, besides.

This was all very easy for Mari, and she soon passed ahead of me in school. In fact, she was so anxious to get to school each day that she would not wait for me. My fingers froze, but Mari had a red fox muff made from probably the only fox Papa ever caught on the River. Mama made it for her, but we had no overshoes nor heavy clothing. Worse than the freezing cold, though, was crossing the Minten pasture with its cattle. My sister was not scared of cattle much, but I had been ever since

Mama had taken me along to the school section the year before to get a herd we had in pasture. A horned cow we'd bought from Louis Pochon was with them, and she charged me. Mama ran in from the side, hollering and waving her apron to scare the cow. The calf was scared most, though, and ran. The cow followed it, and Mama and I were safe, but I never got over my fear.

Then the neighbors got a Galloway bull that must have been fed and fitted, for he was very tame. He would follow us closely across the pasture, probably looking for feed, but I could not stand him so close.

However, the trip to school was not all I had to stand. The girls were usually nice enough to Mari, but I was repeatedly beaten up by the boys. At first, the bigger boys picked on me, until Henry Sandoz, of Great Uncle Paul's family, who was big for his age, put a stop to it because those were older than I. But when the young ones ganged up on me, he thought I should look after myself. All this changed, though, when my brother James started to school. He was a smooth, friendly, charming youngster liked by both the boys and the girls. We soon got a job carrying water to the schoolhouse from the Koller well that was down under the hill by the river. We carried a bucketful every noon and got a dollar a month paid by the teacher. Sometimes the older boys would go along, and we'd all play in Koller's big straw-roofed shed, going hand over hand under the gable crosspieces. James and I were light enough that we could swing on a short hanging rope by our teeth.

In our family, we boys were encouraged to shoot anything from sparrows up that might furnish meat for the table. As soon as I was big enough, I made slingshots, at first small and experimental, but gradually bigger and heavier to handle small rocks. One day, I took my sling-shot to school, and soon all the boys made some. They had me and Marguerite Sandoz, sister of Henry Sandoz and a favorite of mine, go over the bank towards the river to get pebbles for ammunition. Once when they were shooting rocks about the size of pigeon eggs, Marguerite and I came up over the bank, and I got hit in the forehead. It knocked me out and left a small knot on my head that I carried for years. That settled the slingshot business at school.

All in all, this was an excellent school, well-equipped for the times. The teachers, George Peters, and then Mrs. Lathrop, even had a fine model of the universe that they kept locked in a box. Once James found it open and poked his snoopy little head in to see. For years he understood the universe better than I because of that model.

With all her studying at school and staying in at recess to learn more, Mari still had an overflow of enthusiasm for school. By the time I would get home, she would have gone ahead and arranged the chairs in a row somewhat like seats at school. She would have James and Fritz, the baby, seated in line for teaching. Once when she de-manded I take a rear chair, I blew up, and motioning James out with me, we ran to the river to get away. Fritz probably tried to follow for the first time, for we heard a thud and a howl as we left.

In the spring of 1909, we had a big ice jam up the river. It went out one afternoon, and we had just reached the bridge when the water began to swirl over the trash jammed against the bridge railing. One of the four

Ohioans of my sister Mari's book *Old Jules,* Julius Eckerle, saw us on the west side and came down from the house. He forded the water on the bridge and carried us, one at a time, across on his shoulders, Mari first, then me, and finally James. On the last trip, the water was above his waist. I don't know what would have happened if he had not carried us across, because high water and flood that night took out every bridge for twenty miles.

The next fall we had no way to cross the river, since the county commissioners decided not to replace the Sandoz bridge, as it was called. Thus we did not go to school again there regularly, but only occasionally when the temporary footbridge Papa put in was usable. But by then we were somewhat better accepted in the community. One of the boys from school, Joe Koller, took a shine to Mari and came by almost every day, helping us to become part of the neighborhood.

In fact, when it came time for us to move to the Sandhills in 1910, I was completely adjusted and never ceased to miss my "river friends."

Chapter IV

The Surbers Join Us

Life with Papa was never simple, and before we could make the move to the Sandhills, a number of things happened. At the time we started going to the Peters school on the Riverplace about 1904 or 1905, Papa's friend and companion from the Postal Service in Switzerland, Henri Surber, wrote from St. Louis, Missouri. He had seen Papa's name in an advertisement for homesteaders and wondered if it could be his old friend from Zurich. Surber had a wife and three teenage daughters—Elsa, Hannah and Marie. His wife Caroline suffered from migraine headaches, and he thought the change in climate might be good for her. He would like to send his family to Nebraska for the summer with us. Our father was happy at the prospect of seeing the family and told them to come ahead. We calcimined the whole house, including the lean-tos. Everything must be the cleanest possible.

The Surbers were cultured people and soon proceeded to train us in their ways, their manners and their culture. It was a shock when we had to start saying "please" and "thank you." Mrs. Surber was not at all squelched by Papa's rude exterior and felt it her duty to speak up to him whenever she thought it suitable. In the fall the Surbers went back to St. Louis, and the next spring the whole family came. Henri filed on a homestead on Pine Creek southeast of where Uncle Emile Sandoz lived. They stayed with us during the summer, and their wealthy friends, the Goulds, rich from railroading and gold mining in Colorado, came to visit. They brought spicy salami and various other exotic foods that I soon learned to crave.

Someone was upset because the Surbers filed where they did, and one night the first load of lumber they brought out to build a house with, burned. This was on the flat above the creek. So another load was brought out and was unloaded down where water was easily available in case of another fire. This time they watched the lumber closely and quickly had a house built.

Papa was matchmaking, as he sometimes did. He thought the three sons of his brother Emile—Emile Jr., Rudolph, and Fred—would be just fine for the three Surber girls. This did not materialize, and locating Surber there even brought enmity betwen the brothers because now Surber fenced in some free land that our Uncle had considered his pasture.

Another complication arose when Mama's brother, Jake, came from Missouri with a Southern wife. Mama

was already displeased with him, and when she found
that his wife chewed tobacco and could spit in the eye of a
fly across the room, she was really disgusted. My mother
could never accept the pipe smoking and tobacco chewing of Southern women. But Papa was more tolerant and
built them a small house on the Meutsch place on the 160
acres cornering our home place. But they had no staying
powers and soon moved back to Missouri.

The community was fast filling with our relatives and
friends who, unlike Jake, clung tenaciously to the land. It
seems amazing that our father could convince whole
families, even those with small children, to sell everything they had in Switzerland, a fertile, green country of
small farms, precise government, enduring schools, and
meticulous mail service, to come to this country, a raw,
untamed virgin prairie, little government, and no
schools, other than the prospect of establishing some. To
the west on Mirage Flats was his sister Elvina Burrows
and her husband and children Ida, Paul, and John. Southwest a couple of miles was Great Uncle Paul and his wife
"Tante Anna" and children Peter, Felix, Gus, and Jennie
(and more to be born). Great Uncle Gus Sandoz lived a
little west, and near where Uncle Charlie and Aunt Susie
Grossenbacher lived later, two miles east, was Great Uncle Louis Sandoz, his wife, and children Ulysses, Estelle,
Mathilda, Louise, and Numa. Over on Pine Creek were
two of our uncles, the previously mentioned Emile and
Ferdinand Sandoz and his wife. A distant cousin of the
Sandoz family, from Verdigre, was nearby. Our Uncle
William, or "Bill," was on Box Butte Creek that flowed

into the Niobrara above our Riverplace, with the Niobrara fenced off, not to mention the adjacent pastures.

It could only be expected that the cattlemen began to feel threatened, since there were similar encroachments from other sides as well. The Spade Ranch, reputed to have had 500,000 acres of government land fenced in at one time, began to strike back. On the north and east they established big cottonwood groves to indicate ownership, and such plantings as Enlow and Hulls in Cherry County are still identifiable. Dave Tate, presumably a hired killer from Texas, appeared on the payroll. Dan Hill, who had homesteaded to the north, was soon subject to harassment. One time when he was gone, cowboys raced around and around his sod house, shooting in the air. Mrs. Hill cowered inside, under the sod window, with little Fay in her arms.

Grandad Green with his German wife located on the Spade range north of Lakeside. He drove a race mare and stallion around the country. The ranch threatened to tar and feather him, but he felt comparatively safe with his fast team. However, his son-in-law Musfelt was shot while in the field at the plow handles. Subsequent stories were that Tate had stayed at the Hooper ranch throughout the winter, casing the Greens for possible cattle thefts as an excuse.

But when another homesteader, Cole, was shot while visiting with a friend in a hay field in Cherry County, a connection was made with the Spade Ranch and the Johnson County War in Wyoming, since Cole and Musfelt had both been involved there. Mrs. Green sent for Papa to come and stay for a time, which he did, trapping

muskrats and shooting target practice, and the community settled down. Then a settler came to our place with a
bottle containing a rifle shell, considered a warning, he
had found on his doorstep. Papa went to stay with him for
a few days.

With Papa's truck gardening business gone along with
the loss of the Grayson post office, he decided to go into
settling homesteaders on a larger scale. To that end, he
bought a sextant and compass from the county surveyor
for fifty dollars. At first he concentrated on locating
foreigners because at that time homesteading laws were in
favor of emigrants and against native-born sons and
daughters. Foreigners could file on a homestead after
thirty days of filing notice of intent for citizenship, even in
their teens. But Americans had to be twenty-one or heads
of families.

Since Papa could read and write fluently in three lan-
guages and had a working knowledge of several more, he
could and did attract settlers from all over Europe. He
was bringing in endless people to file on free range, to
make homes for themselves and further reduce the available range and water.

Another thorn in the rancher's side was a herd law in
Nebraska stating that anyone's cattle responsible for
damage to crops could be corraled, fed, and watered,
with the owner being liable if notified within twenty-four
hours. This made it difficult to run cattle without a
herder, as all the settlers were soon raising crops. This law
did not always work in practice, but could be very both-
ersome at times.

Of course, we were ruining our own hunting and

trapping with all those settlers coming in. While one year Papa had caught eighty-six otter on Pine Creek and sold the hides for twelve dollars each, now none could be found. People introduced trout into the waters, and those fish ate all the chub fingerlings. Without the chub, the otter disappeared. Papa's only consolation was that now he had neighbors with whom to visit.

In 1904 Moses Kinkaid introduced a bill in Congress that gave homesteaders a right to 640 acres of free land, and it passed. This opened up much arid, marginal territory for settlement, since it had not been possible to make a living on the earlier allocation of 160 of such acres. But with additional land, people would try it. It also provided an opportunity to those who had already used their first homestead allocation to add another 480 acres. But most of this free land was fenced by large ranchers, sometimes covered by fraudulent filings, or concealed by obliterated section corners. Papa looked over the situation on his maps and figured that in our area, the Spade Ranch had most of these places fenced. He also had a grudge against Bartlett Richards, one of the owners, for an incident at Chadron when he was run down by Richards' team on Main Street, and also because Richards was on the jury that found him guilty in the Kollers and Peters shooting case.

Now, following the correspondence with President Teddy Roosevelt and the shooting of Cole and Musfelt, three federal agents arrived at our place. They stayed with us and hired Papa to go to the Sandhills with them to do some surveying, the purpose of which was to map the Spade Ranch and pinpoint the legality of its holdings. He was to go along ostensibly to hunt. On Monday, Mama would prepare a grub box of the whole week's rations. The first week, all three inspectors went. After that, they took turns going out, with one staying at home to do the paperwork. They were very secretive about their activities, but some news did get around.

There were always outsiders around seeking land, but these men were well-dressed and had the air of officers. They didn't look like the average person interested in land. They carried arms out of sight, but we kids knew. Their names were Nixon, Exline (probably not the proper spelling), and an older man, Scott. Scott was a tall man, Exline medium, and Nixon rather short. They kept to themselves when all were there and did not allow us to see their papers. But otherwise they played games with us and guided our principles, helping us to develop. These men came and went rather regularly during good weather for about three years, from 1904 to 1907. So it seems to me we were partly raised by the FBI, or what passed for the FBI at that time.

During their work with our father, they found many destroyed corners. At one place on the Gourley Ranch in Cherry County, an old mower wheel had been buried to sway the compass. Finally Dave Gourley told them about it because he wanted his holdings clarified. When they removed the wheel, many other corners fell into place.

At last the government men went to Omaha, where they prepared a lengthy case against Richards and his partner, Comstock. Papa was called to Omaha as a witness for the case. The owners of the Spade were convicted, and the fraudulent filings were all canceled. That included everything of the ranch except the best hay meadows. Those they had bought in a bona fide manner from the heirs of Civil War veterans who claimed the land with soldier scrip. This scrip was good for any land belonging to the federal government and could be used legally. However, one piece of meadow in the Spade dooryard was overlooked, and the foreman, Mike Petersen, filed on it for himself and proved up. He never did sell to the Spade.

The Richards and Comstock action brought several local townships into public domain. Papa sent out an avalanche of advertising, this time mostly in U.S. publications.

The spring following the departure of the agents, Papa fitted up a spring wagon with provisions, including food, spades, bedding, tent, surveying tools, and on top of everything else, a huge featherbed tied down with ropes, undulating like a half-filled balloon. I went along to see that the team did not run away.

Soon we had continual houseguests, or star-boarders, waiting for their homesteads to be located. Usually the first trip out, the women and children stayed at our house. The next trip they went along to appraise and select a place for the house. Then there were sometimes delays before they could get a house built. This was a learning time for us, exposed to all manner of people. I remember a Mr. and Mrs. Schiller, originally from Austria-Hungary, who stayed with us one whole winter. They were a cultured couple, and well-educated. They sang opera songs for our amusement and tried to teach us the stories as they went along. Another winter the Baum-

gartens came and stayed. They had a pump organ along,
and it was a jolly time with fine singing and playing.
(This organ is in the Sheridan County Historical Museum, given by our sister, Flora Sandoz.)

The George Macumbers stayed overnight with some of their children—Engle, Jennie, and Esther. James and I played hide-and-seek with them. They came from Chadron well-equipped, with two four-horse teams and loaded wagons. They were fun people, Scotch-Irish and talented. (Mari eventually married their eldest son, Wray.) Then there was Charlie Neumeyer. Mama sent him with me to the school section to look after the cattle. He had just come from Europe and was really a greenhorn. When our mean-looking bull bellowed and looked our way, he threatened to throw his gold watch at the animal. I didn't think that would help much, even if it was a fine Swiss instrument. Neumeyer was a tall German with a red mustache who had my sister Mari write his love letters beginning "My Most Heavenly Angel Queen." He still didn't get the lady for a wife.

In one group of settlers were five young men who came from Ohio: Fred Berndt, Andrew Heinz, Cornell Poporada, Julius Eckerle, and a man named Plasco. They played a card game named "Ast" endlessly. Papa got them jobs around the country, and Julius and Fred took homesteads later. Mari made up a short story about Poporada called "Face of the Dying Monk" concerning an unfrocked priest, which he was [published in *The Cottonwood Chest*].

Usually the women in the settler parties were a help to Mama, but some were lazy drifters from Missouri, Oklahoma, and other places, and had small babies. She ended up taking care of the babies and washing their diapers, as she couldn't stand the dirt and the smell.

Of them all, I liked those of East European extraction best for their manners, their gaiety, and their optimistic outlook. Uncle Ferdinand used to come and pick up their actions and accent to entertain us later. He was a natural mimic and comedian. He could stand flat-footed and kick our low ceiling with either foot. But best of all the company, Mama liked the Surbers. She loved the girls, Hannah, Elsa, and Marie, their songs, and the escorts that seemed to accompany them everywhere. Each girl had several admirers, and most of them were of German descent, so the conversation was in her native language with its jokes and sly innuendoes. In the end, most of the foreigners lost out with the girls. Foreign daughters wanted to marry Americans. It was a short-cut to being accepted.

In May, 1906, Papa was off somewhere in the Sandhills for a couple of weeks, and Mama's time came upon her for the birth of another baby. It was May 12, and we had no wood or fuel in the house. James and I were sent off to collect as much as we could to last several days. When we came back, Mrs. Jahn, the local midwife, was there, and we figured something was about to happen. Mama sent us up to Mrs. Surber's to stay for a few days. That good lady was geared to girls, and when she had us help her run the sausage stuffer, we got carried away, winding the handle so fast the sausage shot out through the casing and half-way across the table. We held our sides laughing, but she didn't think it was so funny.

When we got back home, we had another baby in the

family. The memory of Fritz and his bawling did not prepare us favorably for another one, and this was even worse, another girl. But Papa was still not home, and Mari was more pleased than usual and even picked out a middle name, Rose. There were a number of Floras in the community, so it is debatable whether the baby was named for Flora Johansen, but we always thought she was. Anyway, now there were five of us Sandoz children.

Chapter V

Surveying in the Sandhills

Real trouble came to our Niobrara River area in 1908. No one felt really safe when about that time Papa's brother, Emile Sandoz, was shot by Ralph Nieman, a rider who worked for the neighbors up on the Ox-Bow. Nieman had been in the Nebraska region for several years, from Roswell, New Mexico. Our uncle, who lived down the Pine Creek below Surbers, had worked with the rider at the Margrave Ranch, and knew him again at the Schmidts'. Nieman rode into the barnyard and shot Emile in the back while he was branding calves with his sons. Our uncle lived for a couple of days, and the killer vanished.

Emile's family continued to live on the homestead, but his wife Helen was never well again and died within a few years. Both were buried in the Beguin-Swiss cemetery on the flat above their house. The killer eventually was caught in New Mexico, brought back, and convicted. He only served a few years, but that was a precedent, at least.

All this put some caution into our father, who reasoned that he would be the next target because he was locating settlers and doing government surveying to locate free land. In fact, a short while later when he and Pete Sandoz, a son of Great Uncle Paul, attempted to do some locating in the Joy Ranch range, bullets whizzed by, even though the Joys were a very religious family and considered friendly. The two men hid in the wagon box until dark and then drove out of the area and did not go back. Later, Pete located himself more northeast.

When I was eleven years old, I remember Papa needed more horses. From his one horse, Daisy, that Henriette, a former wife, had traded for while he was gone to the Big Horns, we now had one team, Daisy the Second and Billy.

Years before, a wild fox-colored mare joined our herd, and from her we had a mess of young outlaw horses. Gus and Felix Sandoz, Pete's brothers, used to buck them out in our high board corral. This was the corral lumber that Papa had obtained from Johnny Jones in Rushville by trading watermelons. Our neighbors, however, thought he had bought it with the post office money. He had used the post office money, borrowed from Henriette, since he was not the postmaster. But he used that money in a much more imaginative way on a later wife, Emelia.

One time, Marie Surber and other girls were sitting on the board fence gate when the Fox mare jumped over, knocking it and all the girls to the ground. This corral shows on the only photo we have of our old place, taken on the Surber camera. Young Jim Margrave had been to our place several times buying these outlaw horses, but they were nothing we could work. Then Papa bought a livery team, Brownie and Blackie, in Rushville when Frank Waite sold out. Brownie was a darkish brown, with obvious coach blood, probably one of the best horses we ever had. Blackie was not as dependable, and one of her colts became a bucker. Papa then traded six of the broncs for a French coach stallion in Alliance. That horse died in the spring, but we did get several colts from him, one of which was the mare Pacy. She later became foundered and had a permanent limp, but she was our dependable saddle horse for years. Papa kept one stallion colt, but it got out in the Marcy herd and was gelded.

The trips into the Sandhills to survey began to follow a definite pattern. Mama would load the wagon with the heavy Army kettle from the Indians, the bedding, and food—sections of Wisconsin cheese, long four-inch square orange boxes of crackers, home-cured bacon, boughten summer sausage, sardines, coffee, and sugar. Papa would load the canvas tent on top, along with the sextant and compass. He had to give up the featherbed as unmanageable. With the team caught and hitched, we would climb up and sit on the spring seat or the board across the box, whichever we had at the time. I drove if no one else was along, so Papa could be ready to shoot any game that appeared.

On reaching the hills the first time, we had to find an indisputable government corner. We dug on several places for a couple of miles before we were sure of one. Originally they were located at one-mile intervals, marked with four dug holes about four feet apart, in a square, the dirt mounded in the middle on a metal stake. Then ashes were dumped into the holes, which were otherwise left open. These filled gradually with drift sand, and years later could still be identified by the soil marks even if the metal stakes were removed. The first corner we found was at Worena Hill then called Deer Hill by the Indians, who earlier had taken Papa that far and told him not to go beyond it. That was the Land-of-the-Gone-Before-Ones. But he remembered the eighty-seven antelope they shot with as many shells, and he was not about to give in to superstition. So for years, whenever he really had wanted meat after that, he had gone there.

Now the antelope were all gone, and I can't recall seeing any during our locating settler times.

From this Worena Hill, we could sight north and south by compass to start to "chain." The Gunter chain we used was divided on the metric system. A man or boy was at each end of the chain, the lead guy carrying ten stakes with small flags attached, and the rear setting marked by the eleventh stake. In our work, I would go ahead with someone at the back. At the site of the first marking, I called "stuck" and put one stick in the ground. When the back man had reached this, he pulled it up and called "stick." When all stakes were in the hands of the back man, I would stop and wait. Papa would be at the last marked corner waving me north or south, east or west, to true the corner. In this manner, we covered most of the sections in mid-Sheridan County, all four sides.

In his meanderings about the Sandhills, he found a

vacant 480 acres in Township 28, Range 41, near the homestead sites of Pete, Great Uncle Paul and Jennie Sandoz, and he filed on that. He built a frame homestead house on it just southwest of the current Joe Dukat home. In June 1907, Papa and I went to this Sandhills shack, driving Daisy the Second and Billy. The next day the Jeff Orrs, Stanley Forneys, Pete Sandoz, Lloyds, and others met to organize a school district. Since there was not room for everyone inside, the meeting was held outdoors. But they could not get a consensus of opinion for location of the schoolhouse-to-be. Jeff Orr voted with Papa, but the Lloyds wanted it several miles south, as did Stanley Forneys. The location was delayed for another year.

We went over to stay all night with Pete. He had a small tank dug into the ground, really only a hole lined with alkali mud. Lillian, one of Pete's two small daughters, came up behind and pushed me into the tank. She thought it was very funny.

The next summer Papa, with Mari along to look at the house situation, went again to the homestead and over to Pete's to the school meeting to decide on the schoolhouse location. The Lloyds and Forneys had withdrawn and formed another district further south, so it was a simple matter to vote it near the new Strasburger town. On the way home the next day, they stopped at the homestead again. There our father got snakebitten. An October, 1908, issue of the *Rushville Standard* had the following account of the incident:

Jules A. Sandoz was bitten by a rattlesnake Wednes-

day and Dr. Daniel was telephoned for, but was
busy and could not attend the call. Dr. McDowel of
Hay Springs was then sent for and went down to
attend him. Word was received this morning that
Mr. Sandoz would recover.

I remember that it was not Dr. McDowell, but rather
Dr. Shaffner, who came in an automobile. The good
doctor, on leaving, got stuck going west up the River
Hill, and the Surbers had to take their team to pull the car
up the hill when he went back to Hay Springs.

The Strasburger town mentioned above was started by
a lawyer, John B. Strasburger, an uncle to the other
Strasburgers, who came later. He had contacted Papa
through a newspaper advertisement when the Spade
range was opened for settlers. He was a large man, German, with a beard. He stayed with us for a time on the
Riverplace before going back to Chicago to organize a
settler group and make arrangements for their transporta-
tion out. The railroad at that time often granted free, or at
least less expensive, tickets to settlers in order to build up
freight business. This lawyer came back with his Quaker
wife and a group of settlers, including the three single
Dowd ladies, two McMillans (piano tuners) and their
families, Miss Hughes (a music teacher), Mr. and Mrs.
Starr (storekeepers), Mrs. Poole and Mr. Hardison, both
of whom later ran boarding houses; Bill, Walter, and Ida
Philpott; Sara Roadifer, who later married Fred Berndt;
and Dr. Schoch.

Papa had helped Strasburger locate a block of land
which he was able to survey into smaller homestead units

for these people and for himself. He hired the McMillans to carry mail and established a post office in his large sod house, which he hoped would later become the hub of a Strasburger town complete with a railroad. A Ladies' Aid was soon organized, and it was instrumental in building a large sod structure to be used as a Sunday School, church, public library, and meeting house.

After the snakebite, Mari no longer went along locating settlers. Papa would be sleeping out with men, some rough, even by his standards, so I went.

It seemed to me all the demons in the world were on those trips. There were wailing birds piping around the lakes at night—black, black nights with no light except the cowchips and grass smudge. But it gave me a different view of Papa and an opportunity to gauge men, to hear their rough talk, and to learn surveying. I don't recall that we ever had any trouble on these trips. I was willing to obey exactly, since it involved our living, and in those days it seemed to me hunger was always with us. Later, our father lost the Snakebite place because a government man, not connected with the Secret Service at our place on the River, found the house unoccupied. We could not tell him of the government secret work that held up our moving, so the place went to Miss Hughes of Strasburger's settlement.

When Papa had been locating blocks of land for Strasburger and Alexander Hamilton, another Chicago lawyer, he noticed a 480-acre tract of free land north and east of the Snakebite spot. This tract ran into the lake country of the Margrave Ranch, and part of one lake lay on it, according to a preliminary sighting with the compass. Upon finding this land where ducks and geese could be shot, he was happy not to fight the cancellation of the last homestead in a dry area. He would regain his right to file and use it again. Hunting was one of the most important things in his life anyway.

When we located the Hebberts and Drurys in Range 41, Township 28, I sometimes rode a sorrel stallion belonging to the Hebberts. Its name was Scott, a big horse, probably originated from the Fort Robinson herd, as the Hebberts were from nearby Whitney. There were two brothers, Harry and John, blacksmiths. Jess Brewer, a relative, had come along to help with the horses, cattle, and tools. They had a big tent at Harry's temporary place near a Spade windmill, located supposedly on deeded land. The survey, however, disclosed that the well was not on the Spade, but actually on Hebbert's filing, which was indeed a windfall for that settler.

One day we were surveying at the Cherry County line, and Drury was at the rear end of the chain. I carried the lead with the ten stakes, with Papa sighting and guiding me with arm signals from a pile of sod at a government corner. We were surveying "Big Hill" on the north of John Hebbert's prospective homestead. Upon attainment of that fierce climb, we were pretty well fagged out, me pulling the chain and sometimes seemingly pulling Drury, too. I took bearing and decided on a certain place for the next corner, when Papa signaled us to return. Drury, being roly-poly, suggested we roll down the hill. The grade was steep, the dry sand sloped down smooth as a board. He rolled very well, but I didn't. I was lean and encumbered with the chain folded and with stakes and straps about it. This was the condition of the hills when I first saw them, whole slopes with no grass at all.

Drury and Brewer decided they had better have their homesteads resurveyed, so Papa did that for fifteen dollars per homestead. They found that Brewer's house, already built on a previous trip, was not on his land at all and had to be moved. Later we heard he married a mail-order bride as many, many settlers did, and eventually left the country. Descendants of the Hebberts and Drurys are still around.

When settling ordinary prospects from scratch in the Sandhills, not like the Hebberts, who had brought themselves, the charge was twenty-five dollars. We might go to Lakeside to meet the families, or they might have come to our place on the River on a previous day. Together, the next day, we'd go to look at an intended homestead, in their conveyance or our wagon. Papa would always see to it that the place had some level ground for farming and also some nearby neighbor with a common origin or religion or interests, so they would be happier and more apt to stay to become permanent residents.

After a satisfactory place had been found, we drove to Lakeside, left the team and wagon at the livery stable, and took a train caboose for fifty cents paid to the brakeman, to Alliance to make a filing at the land office. Sometimes we stayed at a hotel, but occasionally we stayed with Frank Broome, the federal land man, or with other friends. Papa would give me some small coins to go to a show or roller-skating, but I did not care for any story made up, nor the strangers at the rink, so usually went about town looking and listening. I liked it best, though, if I could stay in Lakeside, and I learned to know that town very well.

Sometimes we would be looking over the hills with no one along, and then we'd try to reach some settler's home before dark. Papa never asked if we could stay; we just did. I was embarrassed and thought we were not always welcome, but he'd carry in some game, a few grouse or rabbits to be sure there was food enough. If we did not reach a place, we pitched our tent and boiled water for coffee. He'd put a half-inch of strong settler-made butter in the iron Army kettle to pot-roast game for supper and breakfast. We lived mostly on meat.

In our wanderings, I often carried fish from the Riverplace or Pine Creek in a syrup can hung from the ring of the end-gate rod. If we drove all day and the water got too hot, it killed the fish. I now wonder at Papa's patience at my changing water at every reservoir and tank we encountered. It was my "humbug" he said, but I made it through with enough live fish to stock many of the rising lakes. It paid off in many a fishfry in later years.

Chapter VI

Camping in the Osborn Valley

Papa recovered from the snakebite of 1908, but he always carried the big white scar where he'd shot the swelling off. He'd just missed the tendons on the back of his left hand, so still had good use of his fingers for gunsmithing.

In the spring of 1909, he and I went to the Sandhills to his new 480-acre homestead on Sections 19 and 30, Range 41, and Township 28, and pitched our tent in the Osborn Valley a mile north of what is now the Sandoz orchards next to Margrave Ranch land. This valley already had a tragic history years old. County records show that it was homesteaded in 1893, some sixteen years earlier, by a family named Osborn. This couple had two little boys. They built a sod house near a swamp of dense rushes and tall cane. One fall a big prairie fire came along, and the parents knew they had to fight it, so they locked the two sons in the sod house where they would surely be quite safe, and left. When they had the fire out and returned,

the boys were not in the house. They called and called,
but there was no answer. Evidently the little ones had
found a way out of the house and, being frightened by the
smoke, ran into the swamp. The parents found them
there, suffocated. The loss was too much, and the couple
left the homestead, and the Margraves took over. We
never heard of Leonard and Alice Osborn again.

When we got to our destination, we pitched our tent
just east of a small lake in the west end of the valley and
east of a prairie dog town. We called it Alkali Lake, but it
has long since been drained and is grassed over. This was
in a meadow a short way from the Spade range where
Papa looked at the grass and decided there would be water
at about three feet. We dug a four-foot-square hole, but
didn't hit water until much deeper, maybe ten feet. We
had no lumber along, so could make no curbing. About
two barrels of water a day would seep into this well. Later
in the summer when Margraves hayed, they corralled
their horses about a half mile east in a hundred-foot sod
enclosure. We could always remember in later years
where their corral was because mushrooms usually grew
large as dinner plates in the decaying sod.

Sam Speer came over to plow for us, and in the evenings Papa would build a grass smoke inside the tent to
keep the mosquitoes out. They were terrible. He and Sam
sat inside the tent and told tales way into the night. Our
plowman had been in Alaska, and I wanted very much to
hear the stories, so I lay on the tent flap where a little
smoke oozed out, and where I thought the rattlesnakes
would not be likely to venture. I learned from Sam's
stories on that trip how men behave when there is a

scarcity of women. That was the first I'd heard of that subject, and much later it was well I had.

The morning after Speer's arrival, he and Papa attempted to put together a sod-buster plow. They had a breaking plowlay that had to go on a stirring plow, from Pochon. Speer had worried in the night how this could be done, since the holes for the bolts did not match. But Papa had had lots of experience with plows. The government had sent him one to try, one with a heavy beam and two-foot-deep chisels called a stubble plow. We never had a team that could pull it. Another kind, backset plows, were used mostly for plowing fireguards. They made blow-outs in every field where used. So the breaking plow was essential. Papa had Speer line up the two plowshares, the breaking and the stirring, and backing off a few inches, he shot through the breaking plowshare with his rifle, making a neat hole. Together they assembled the plow. Sam said, "Who but Old Jules Sandoz would ever have thought of that." Speer stayed most of two months and made enough to pay for a horse.

When we finished the survey for the north fence so Speer would know approximately where to plow, he made a round and put a jug of whiskey under a sod in one corner where he stopped on succeeding rounds to rest his team. He had three horses, two of which he'd hired from his brother, Al Speer, for a dollar a day, and a blind horse he owned. He planned to work every day. With him plowing, Papa and I proceeded to build a fence through the Alkali Lake that had filled from two winters of heavy snow. The water was milky white from alkali and contained tadpoles and salamanders (water puppies). Before

we had the well dug, that's the water we'd used for coffee.
After screening, we'd fill a pail to within an inch of the top, add coffee and much sugar, and bring it to a boil to kill the smaller vermin not screened out. I had to remember that some children at the Joy Ranch had died from alkali poisoning. The water in the well was a little better later, but still had to be boiled. One morning the blind horse fell into the well, and we had to dig a trench to lead him out.

We found we could not wiggle the fenceposts into the bottom of the lake as we had done on the Niobrara in the quicksand. We had to dig a hole with an auger through three feet of water. Next, the wood posts would not stay down. That was remedied by inserting sixteen foot-long ash posts we'd brought along. The weight held them down. But this killed time, aad our posts looked strange when I saw the slim osage ones shipped in from Preston, Nebraska, by the Margraves. We stopped, too, to plant sod corn with a jerk planter. Bill Sears, who had wandered down to see what we were doing, stayed and helped us some.

As the summer heat came on, the Spade cattle came in big herds, because after the rancher prosecutions, their wells were abandoned, and a few local settlers had the cattle in herd and were to take care of them. But there were no fences and no water west of our place until Pine Creek, over fifteen miles away. One afternoon the cattle broke the fence down and ate all of the corn. Then later, we would see those big rangy Texas steers on windy days running down the rolling Russian thistles. They would put one front hoof on the weed and hold it down while eating. Nebraska cattle were not smart enough to do this. After the corn was gone, and we had the fence replaced, Papa sent Comstock of the Spade Ranch a bill for $155 and got a check right back for damages, with a request for advice on planting an orchard in the middle of Ellsworth. This orchard shows nicely on a picture of the town in about 1912.

It was about this time that Papa went on a locating trip by himself, past Julius Eckerle and Fred Berndt, to get some other Germans settled. He had a runaway that demolished the wagon, so he led his wagonless team into the Spade Ranch and borrowed a yellow-wheeled buggy from Comstock to get home. In fact, he kept the buggy so long that one day when he met the local mail carrier, that public servant was aghast and asked how he came to have it. Papa explained, and the carrier said that was supposed to be his mail-carrier buggy. So our father took the buggy back. Comstock was always friendly; it was only Bartlett Richards who was so annoying.

Perhaps it was on that same trip that I heard later Papa finally lost his patience with one of his "settlers." This man in particular was irritating anyway, and after being shown about four different possible locations in the Tom Roethler area, the fellow still wasn't satisfied. Papa drove over to the telephone line leading from Walter's Lake to Ellsworth, about twelve miles, stopped his team and ordered, "Get the hell out and walk; the railroad is straight down that telephone line; you can't miss it."

Soon there were more prospective homesteaders around again, and we both went locating. Later in the summer we returned, and I went down in the brush patch

on Margrave's to pick wild currants, both yellow and
black, and chokecherries that grew sweeter there than in most places. I was glad to meet the Drury family again, picking also. And they had walked two miles. Their father was working for the Spade Ranch, and they told me that one morning after a storm, they found their saddle horse dead in a corner of the pasture, killed by lightning. I thought of one of Mama's sayings: "Only those who have, can lose." It was their only horse.

Many more settlers had moved into our area during the spring and summer. There were the Craigs, Cooks, and Hoaglands, all an intermingled family of in-laws and cousins. The Cooks did not have wives: Dave, Sam, Bill, and the father Ira, all bachelors, with homesteads each. The Craigs consisted of Dave, Bill, Newt, and their families. Hoagland's wife was a Craig. These people were brought up from Richardson County in southeast Nebraska by the Margrave Ranch to take filings ostensibly for the ranch interests. But when they proved up, many sold to the Strasburgers. However, the land was scattered among the Margrave meadows to which the ranch held deeds for many years.

One day we had run out of bread when the Spade windmill man, Craig, came by. It was Saturday evening, and he was on his way home to a Margrave house on one of their hay camps a mile around the hill from us in the Jacobs Valley. He said to come to his house for bread. The next morning Papa sent me over there. When I knocked, someone called to come in. I learned when I went in that a daughter was just dressing and supposed it was a sister knocking for a joke. It was embarrassing because she was in her petticoat. But Mrs. Craig came in and said they were out of bread, too, so she fried us both some quick bread in a skillet.

Once more we had to go back to the Riverplace to winter. And we were ill-prepared. One way and another, my folks had built up a herd of one hundred head of cattle. But Papa had no idea at all of how to run cattle. Instead of taking care of the herd and securing hay on the River, he'd expected to be in the Sandhills feeding the corn the Spade cattle had eaten. He still could have used the check from Comstock to buy feed, but he had no idea that way. He expected to get by on the seventeen acres of cornshocks that Mama and Emil Schoen had bound by hand.

We abandoned our camp in the Osborn and went home. I got there in time to help Mama harvest the onions, and there were a lot of them. For once, Papa had listened to his cousin-in-law on his mother's side and had planted the onion seed without plowing the ground first. This hard ground proved ideal. This cousin-in-law, who most of the Sandoz family called crazy even though he was not, was the husband of a woman that Papa got along with well, a sixth cousin. Anyway, I helped harvest the onions since Andy Brown, who'd been hired for the job, was gone as usual. But now the cart that James and I had pulled two years before with our chests, was pulled by a rope from our saddle horse through the deep sand up the hill a half mile to the house. We had more than a wagon-load of onions, about eighty bushels.

But we lost about thirty head of the hundred cattle that winter. Mama was expecting another baby to be born in May, and she was unable to work as much as usual. I did what I could, but the cows were so weak many got down sometime during the winter and could not get up. And even if they did manage to get around, they had to go to water on the river and would get down in the quicksand. When Papa got done selling the next fall, we had twenty-eight head left.

As it was, we had to try to go back to the Peters school. Papa arranged a footbridge. The main thing I remember of that winter was that I discovered girls. I was about twelve. So far our sister Mari had just been a bossy someone that James and I had to contend with. But when I met Floy Alderman in school, I was smitten and remembered her for many years, although I did not see her again after we moved. I'm sure she did not know I existed. I thought, too, that Marguerite Sandoz was very interesting, but Mama pointed out that she was a relation and not to be anything but a good friend. I cannot remember after that winter any time when I did not think girls were something special.

The Tom Taylor children, Helen and Jim, entered school with us that winter. Often Jim would take me up behind him on his horse, and those days I did not walk home from school. I remember that Etta Peters (Shipp) was the smartest in school and could usually answer all the questions. Maggie Peters was exceptionally good at baseball, in contrast to me. I was so poor in athletics, they put me in the outfield with two or three girls. Mari was the tallest girl in school that year and was entranced with our teacher, Mrs. Lathrop. But it was a year of children's diseases. Measles and mumps plagued all of us. However, since Mama had worked for a doctor in St. Louis, she knew quite a bit about nursing. We came through it all right, but one of the Peters girls died. I remember her so well; it was very sad.

One day in early winter when Mama and I were running Papa's mink traps while he was gone hunting, we found one caught. Mama couldn't kill anything. We tried to drown the animal, but it would come to life every little while, and we'd beat it on the head so as not to spoil the hide. After that, I carried a .22 rifle along to kill the game. That same winter James and I trapped muskrats on Staskwiecz' pond, made where he'd drained the river.

Towards spring, Mama had gone across the Niobrara to look after the cattle. The ice was going out, and she was too awkward to get back, having a baby due in a couple of weeks. John Peters came along and took her by the arm to help her across the ice floes. We boys were becoming knowledgeable now, and later when Walter Flueckinger came and took James and me on his horse to his home, we were quite sure we would have another baby in the family. This time Mrs. Surber was the midwife, and two weeks later when the census man came around and our baby sister had no name, she was called "Caroline" after Mrs. Caroline Surber. Now we were six in the family.

Chapter VII

Move to the Sandhills

After our sister, Caroline, was born on May 21, 1910, Papa and I began making plans to go to the Sandhills homestead again, twenty-two miles into the hills. Mama and the rest of the family would stay on the Riverplace for the summer. Since Mrs. John Sears and Mrs. Flueckinger would come by probably every week going to town, usually stopping for dinner, Mama could send to town for necessities. As soon as the juneberries would be ripe, she would have money.

On our way in the loaded lumber wagon, for we had all the tools necessary to build a house, we stopped for dinner at the Fred Beguin home on Pine Creek. Papa had bought a big load of Washington white pine lumber in Hay Springs, so he hired Fred to haul it out with his four-horse team. When we reached the homestead, which was called Sowers Valley for a man who had homesteaded there in the nineties, we had no water because there was no lake there. We'd found the previous year in surveying that our camp in the Osborn was on Margrave land, so we'd moved over the hill south. This was a long valley sloping east from a prairie dog town, a half mile wide and ending two miles away at what we now call Bootlegger's Hill in the east. To the west, it ended between the folds of a vast "V."

We started an open well at once in the middle of the flat, and when we got down about four feet, we struck hardpan, a thick dry clay almost as hard as cement. I was working in a four-foot-square hole without much space, so Papa cut off the handle of an ax for me, and I chopped the way down four or five feet deeper. Papa was making a wood lining called a curbing and settling it in the hole as we went so the dirt would not cave in. He pulled up the clay and sand to empty on a pile until water began seeping in. At fourteen feet, we reached a pretty good layer of mud and water, so I nailed two-by-fours across one side and crawled out. We fitted a windlass and water bucket to lift water for the horses and poured it into a shallow basin made of the hard clay I'd chopped.

In a few days, Beguin arrived with the lumber, and by now Papa had been in Alliance and brought out a bum he'd picked up starving in a railroad yard. Elias Worena was an Eastern European, probably of Bulgarian, Slav, and Croatian mixture, and talked a broken kind of English. He'd worked his way from Europe on a ship crossing the ocean around South America, then north, docking in Washington state. He hopped a freight car there and got locked in. He'd not eaten for three days when the train crew found him in Alliance. The station agent contacted our father, who took him to breakfast and brought

him out to our camp. Fortunately, he was somewhat of a
carpenter and understood how to make a hip roof.

Papa hired Curt Wilson to plow the valley land for three dollars an acre for alfalfa where there was a tangle of buckbrush and rosebushes. But first he plowed five acres where the buildings were going to set so they wouldn't burn in a prairie fire.

Worena helped lay out the store building. We would live in that until more lumber could be brought out. They cut all the rafters and laid them out on the ground. Local riders drifting through swore it would never work, that you couldn't build a roof like that. But it did work, and when erected, the pieces fit so well it was almost as if they had grown so. In fact, it was the only building on the place that never leaked, and it stands there seventy-two years later solid and strong, as part of the old house in the East Garden, a building much admired by tourists.

We had not had much rain that spring, and Curt Wilson had a terrible time plowing. The buckbrush roots were so big, we pulled them by hand to use for fuel. The ground was so dry, Wilson, pessimist that he was, said all the seed would be thrown away. But when the plowing was done, the Kicken brothers, Louis and Frank, arrived looking for homesteads. Papa said the seed must go in first, since Wilson was hired to cover it with a disc, and that man wanted to finish and go back to his own homestead about six miles west.

The Kickens were Hollanders by way of France, where they had married French women. They had been in this country earlier at Hemingford, where they'd worked on the railroad. There they dug wells two hundred and fifty feet deep by hand. But they got homesick and had gone back to France for a few years. Now they were in America again with another man along, Paul Job, who had followed the family, since he was interested in one of the daughters. When they were here before, there had been four brothers. The other two, Pierre and William Kicken, had gone to Deadwood, South Dakota, where the former had bought the Keystone Hotel. William worked there as a night clerk in the 1880s. Pierre married one of the maids, who had a small daughter, and together they moved back to Hemingford, where he became one of the first tractor farmers in Box Butte County. William married a North Carolina girl and raised a daughter, who was the girl I later married.

The Kickens decided to help plant the alfalfa to speed things up. Next morning, Louis and I started out. He was carrying and operating a hand planter called a cyclone seeder, and I was carrying the refill sack of Turkestan seed. After a few rounds, Louis complained his feet hurt and went to the house. Frank put the seeder over his shoulders, and together we covered the rest of those twenty-three acres. I walked every round carrying the sack of seed imported from Russia. Wilson came right behind us with the disc, and we were just finished in the afternoon when a two-inch rain came. Later, every seed seemed to have grown, even those not covered where the ground was so rough and the buckbrush stuck out. The little roots made it into the ground someway and produced clusters of shoots.

Then Papa went with the Kickens to find land. I did not get to help on that survey, because I had to stay and watch the homestead to comply with filing rights. When he

came back, I'd been alone for two weeks. He had found
enough land in one locality north of Lakeside for the three
brothers and Job. Pierre did not come along. Papa made
several more trips to Alliance to the land office and then
came back to get me. I went along, and the Kickens gave
me a job herding their cattle that watered at a Spade mill.
The ranch cattle would come in, drink, and run away,
taking my herd along, and, although I had a saddle horse,
still it was a hard job. I could not talk to any of the family
excepting a daughter who spoke English, Helen Jean,
when she was home.

On the Fourth of July, we were back on the homestead,
and in the morning I picked wild currants. Omar West, a
neighbor, was doing some more sod-breaking for Papa.
He lived over a hill southwest. We had not located him;
the Spade had. That day his wife and two daughters,
Olive and Pearl, ten and twelve, came over so they could
make him some dinner, since he was working on the
Fourth. I was making currant jelly in a boiler when they
came, and Mrs. West thought me rather odd to be making jelly. After looking at my runny jam, she suggested
that I needed more green currants to make it jell. She
didn't know I didn't want stiff jell; I wanted syrup. The
Wests were relatives of the Croffutts whom Papa had
located a few years before in the Spade range.

Their land joined ours, cutting off a hundred sixty
acres of deeded Spade land from their school section in
the Four-Inch-Mill pasture south. There had been an old-
time watering place in their pasture with two large wells
and a hundred-foot reservoir made of earth many years
before. West leased his land to the Spade and later sold to

them, so they had no immediate worry, and even though our homestead lay on three sides of their deeded land, the fences were never changed. (When the Spade sold out in the 1920s, we were able to buy both the West place and the lease of the school section.)

I planted corn behind the neighbor's breaking plow with a jerk planter: step, plant, step, plant. I liked West, him being a genuine Missouri Yankee, handy at most anything. When the Spade found out that he was plowing for us with a team he'd borrowed from them, they called for their horses back. My father wrote to his old friend and neighbor Elmer Sturgeon, south of Hay Springs, and enabled West to buy a team with no down payment. Elmer had one of the largest horse farms in Nebraska—good horses, large imported French stock. When their father finished his plowing, the girls soon were riding these fine Percheron mares, Mimi and Mollie, bareback around the community.

All this time, Mama was with the rest of the family on the Riverplace. She was not well, and when she could, got Mari to help can fruit, as there was a bumper crop, besides selling to the Peters, Kutcheras, Heitings, and other neighbors. That was the summer, I think, that Albert Modisett used to come past from his ranch in a top buggy and buy a couple of quarts of cherries to take to Ida Marcy. But either she didn't like long-stemmed Dyehouse cherries or taciturn Modisett; anyway, she married Jamison of Lakeside, instead.

Papa had more lumber brought, and through July and August, we built a series of five rooms, lean-to's like those behind the Riverplace house, Papa's favorite kind of carpentry. He didn't need a ladder, which he couldn't climb with his bad ankle anyway. He could stand on the ground and reach the roof. The whole building was a series of descending depressions for floors. The walls were of foot boards, both inside and outside of the two-by-four studs. We filled the spaces with alkali mud from a puddle that had gathered below the house and the well-diggings in the big rain. Papa hired another Wilson, no relation to Curt that I know of, to make bricks for the chimneys, one for the center of the store, and another for the kitchen. Wilson's home and kiln were south about fifteen miles by Alvah Hamilton's place, halfway to Ellsworth. There was a particularly strong alkali mud there that made up into fairly satisfactory bricks.

Wilson brought the bricks, and Papa laid up the chimneys on two-by-ten-inch bridge planks, upright about five feet and topped with the brick chimneys in both the store and our twenty-four-by-fourteen-foot kitchen. This was all the heating system for our five-room house and store. The descending rooms that were even deeper in the ground consisted of the kitchen–living room with an ell for a semi-private bedroom for the girls, and a shop on the northeast, one-windowed with north and south side benches and no outlet for smoke from the forge, excepting a door into the kitchen. Surely it would be a brooding source of irritation for the family in coming years when Papa would be welding and brazing. Papa's bedroom joined the shop on the west, with another room west of that. Finally, there was a twenty-four-by-four-teen-foot potato room, with no windows at all and a pit dug in the center.

On August the 25, Papa brought James and Mari (p.

350, *Old Jules*) from the Riverplace to stay on the home-stead, and that day I rode Kit, the fleabitten gray mare Mari had ridden down, back to the old home. The horse had been Henriette's, Papa's second wife's. There had been a heavy frost that night, which froze everything. I'd been gone since the first of June and was shocked when Mama kissed me. I'd thought better of her.

With James gone for the first time, it left Fritz alone and confused. He had lost his anchor. One day he did not come home from a walk, and towards evening, I followed his tracks through the orchard and across the river to Spring Creek and found him where Grandma Fehr had had her homestead. He was just seven.

Fortunately, after the early frost we had a long and pleasant fall, and Mama and I pulled and flailed the dry beans and field peas. The weather held until almost the first of November, when we finally got ready to move. Bill Cook, a plump and good-natured neighbor from the Sandhills, and Bill Sears came horseback to help me move the cattle. Mrs. Jim Cerny, aunt of Bill Sears and wife of the Convict Jim, came to drive the team for Mama. They had canned goods, bedding, cooking utensils, everything all loaded in the lumber wagon box, for everything possi-ble must be moved or considered abandoned. Mama sat on the wagon seat with six-months-old Caroline in her arms. Fritz and Flora sat on boxes in the wagon bed as they started.

We turned the twenty-eight head of cattle out of the corral to follow, but these cows did not want to leave the only place they knew, and only after considerable turning and running could we three riders get them started over

the hill towards our new home. At last they started to
follow the wagon, and I looked back from the Charley
Sears hill, the last rise into the Sandhills, with a catch in
my chest. I thought never again would we hear the
friendly church bell from the Sacred Heart belfry across
the river, never ride with the Taylors or watch Joe Koller
as he turned in beside the asparagus patch. I could not
understand Papa's thinking. Here he had five quarter-
sections of land, three boys getting big enough to farm, a
decent enough house, plenty of water in the Niobrara,
and a fruit orchard bearing heavily apples, cherries,
plums, and even pears, the big Flemish pears growing
well back on the chalk cliff. Many trees were fifteen years
old and in their prime. And now to move to the Sandhills
of antagonistic ranchers, no fruit, no running water, and
neither school nor post office. Maybe he'd just run out of
things to fight about on the river.

But the cattle did not give us much time to think. We
tried to keep them along with the wagon or along a fence
when possible, past the Tallon and Bolek homesteads.
Fortunately, Bill Sears knew every hill and valley because
he and his brother Walter and his mother Sophie rode and
raced their horses everywhere. We all stopped at noon for
a short rest at a Modisett windmill, but it became a long
day, and the cattle tired as we neared our Sandhills home.
But that is all that kept them from being swept away by a
big herd of Spade steers. As it was, we whooped and
hollered, and finally Cook and Sears drove the steers over
a hill, while I held our cows together. It was surely with
vast relief that we entered the west end of our home valley
at dusk and could see ever so faintly the kerosene light
flickering through the window. On reaching the yard, we

bedded the cattle down in a small corral Papa had built north of the house. Cook, Sears, and I unsaddled our horses, turned them out into the pasture, and walked wearily to the house. Mama and Mrs. Cerny had reached the new place earlier and, with Mari, had made supper for all of us.

As we sat down, ten of us, at the old scroll-legged table from the river kitchen, with baby Caroline in her high chair, I thought of the last two years of batching and going back and forth between the two places. At last here we were, all together again.

Chapter VIII

The Sandhills Orchards

After our sunny south-facing house on the river, Papa's Sandhills home was a gloomy place. With only a half-window in the kitchen east, and a single-wide double one in the living west end—the store was on the south—there was scarcely even enough light to read by, especially in winter. And by the time we got settled, it was winter. We had always had brush to cut for fuel along the Niobrara, but now we faced the cold unprepared. When the snow came and we could not find cowchips, James and I would go to the Osborn and cut the tops off those long ash poles Papa and I had sunk in the mud in the alkali. We dragged them home horseback and cut them up in the kitchen with a bucksaw, one of us at each end. Of course, we were never warm. But no one ever considered getting coal. For one thing, our horses were too played out from the moving and could not have hauled the wagon to town empty. So we wore our coats and extra clothes all day in the house, as well as outdoors. Mama had two big knitted shawls, one black and one white wool, very soft, that Grossmutter had brought from Switzerland. She kept Caroline wrapped in those. All one could see was a runny nose sticking out of the covers. Fortunately, it was not a bad winter.

When we were settled, the next consideration was that of school. Mari was agitating, for she was fourteen and only in the fifth grade, and we three boys were all of school age. We tried to attend the newly established Hebbert school after New Year. I drove the team hitched to a two-wheeled cart carrying Mari, James, and Fritz. We were soon informed that the teacher had contracted for just so many pupils to teach, us not included, and besides, the schoolhouse was too crowded.

With cattle, we needed a more adequate watering system than a mud basin. Curt Wilson and his brother wanted to put down a sand-bucket well, which was quite common then, and depended on the churning action of sand and water inside a wellpipe. But Heywood happened along with a drilling outfit operated by one horse on a walk-around, so he was hired to do the job. The well, when finished, was only about thirty-eight feet deep with the pipe sticking up in a six-foot well-hole. Papa tried to assemble the brass cylinder, but the leathers had too small a hole. So I was sent horseback on Brownie, leaving her colt at home, to the Hebberts to get a larger set. They did not have any, but took time to ridicule my saddle horse with her snaffle bit and sweaty hide from trying to turn back to her colt. When I got home, Papa took the shotgun and reamed out the leathers, as he had

done with the plowshare the year before. Only, the first
shot was too close; the hole was still too small. So he
backed off further and took another shot. We made a
wooden tower and put up a wooden-wheeled Dempster
windmill. Since there were no trees around, as soon as we
had a well working, I stuck a cottonwood slip in the wet
ground. It grew fantastically, branched nicely with shiny
leaves, and soon the cats had something to climb, and
Caroline could look up longingly for her pals.

In the spring of 1911, our first in the hills, Papa started a
vast orchard project. Ordering several thousand trees, he
hired Arthur Tucker to plow twenty acres on the hillside
across south from the house, another seven acres, called
the East Garden, against the north hill, and a big garden
west of the house. Then he moved his plowman over the
hill south and plowed another fifteen acres behind John
Strasburger's homestead sodhouse. This latter would be
put in rye for a year.

The Kickens freighted out the trees from Lakeside, all
well-packed in eight-foot-long wooden boxes, with
damp moss and excelsior. The trees arrived live and in
good condition. Papa planned to sell enough to pay for
his own, but of course, that did not happen. A few people
like Mrs. Beckler bought some because the Florence crab
apples carried her first name, or for some other sentimen-
tal attachment.

Papa had no idea of systematic planting so the rows
could be cultivated both ways. He did not care how
difficult anything would become. He made a plat and
started willy-nilly, merely stepping off the distances east
and west, but the distances between the rows was exact
and exceedingly straight. We dipped water from the bar-

rel by the house and carried it to the orchard. Papa pruned, consulted his map, and debated with himself. The neighbors and the family, chiefly the family, dug holes, planted, tamped, and watered. In the patch across the valley, there was a big block of short rows of Wragg sour cherries across the top, with longer rows of apples, some summer, fall, and winter, and plums below. We were under pressure to finish before the trees started growing or the moss dried out. The East Garden became an experimental patch with cooking pears, Dyehouse and Montmorency cherries, and Wyant plums with berries between.

When the planting was finished, my parents took the family, excepting me, and went to the Riverplace to care for the orchard there. They found the windows shot out, gates down, and strange cattle in our pastures. The house had been stripped, every one of the toys from Uncle Paul that Fritz had not torn apart was gone, along with anything else moveable. Papa hired the Kozals to help hoe the trees for that week. Then the family came back, leaving Mari and James to finish the hoeing, and to can and sell the fruit when it ripened. They were left a saddle horse for going to the Colclesser Flour Mill on Pine Creek for groceries when necessary.

Without Mari to look after the smaller girls, Mama could not do much outside, so Papa hired the Squires family, the Tuckers, and anyone else available, and with their help, Fritz and I hoed those trees the second time. Fortunately, trees take less care the first year or two, since it is possible to plow right up to the tiny trunks. But Fritz

Jules Alexander Sandoz, Jr.
First son of Old Jules

Mary Fehr Sandoz with Jules, Jr., four years; James, three years, and Mari, five years. Taken in 1901 by Surber camera in Sandoz orchard, northwest Nebraska

The Jules Sandoz home on the Riverplace sometime before 1910. Mari, Jules, James, Fritz, Flora, and Caroline were all born in this house. Note tall board corrals in background, garden in front, and milk cow staked at side. Looking west across the Niobrara River. Photo by Surbers.

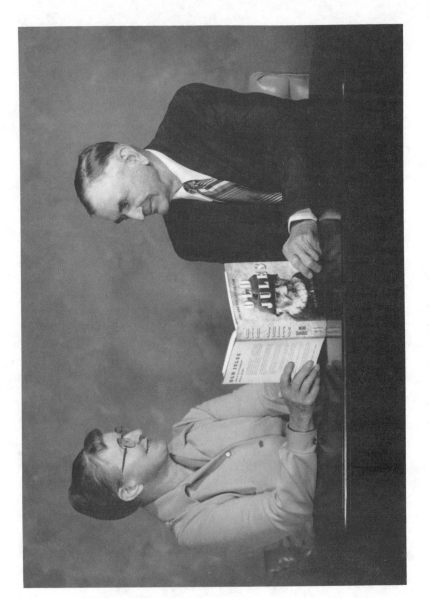

Caroline Sandoz Pifer and brother Jules Sandoz, Jr., in 1978

was little help and continued to be so for the next fifteen
years, until he went out on his own. No amount of
prodding could overcome the first years of his coddling.
He made hot beds and raised flowers.

We lost many friends on moving from the Riverplace,
and we had to make a whole new circle. Papa put in a
stock of essentials, happily making out orders to Butler
Brothers of Chicago for dress goods, overalls, shirts, and
socks; to Kirkendalls for shoes; to Wright and Wilhelmy
for forks, rakes, hoes, spades, nails, and staples, as well as
lamp chimneys and lanterns; and lastly, to Paxton and
Gallagher for groceries: tobacco, gum, coffee, and candy
in big wooden buckets of assortments in bulk, as well as
tea delivered in the original lead packings from the
Orient.

Because of the supplemental income from the orchard
on the river, Papa was able to extend credit. The settlers
arrived in wagons, on horseback, and on foot. Our store-
keeper father would stake anyone to ten, fifteen dollars'
worth of groceries, some much more. In return he was
able to get land plowed, freighting done, buildings made,
and he acquired sheets and sheets of names of deadbeats as
well as honest folks. But we were no longer lonesome.
Every sandhill pass to our place soon became a drifting
sand dune. The settlers had little to do, were bored, and
coming to our store became a pastime. Arthur Tuckers
came almost every day, as did Cooks, Craigs, Wray
Macumber, the Squires family, Kindigs, Duncan Mc-
Allister, all representatives of the lavish turnout for the
land bonus Kinkaid had staked them to. They became our
confidantes, playmates, and companions. The Schoen-

felts brought us their stereopticon slide views to help pass time; others entertained us with match tricks, riddles; others just brought gossip.

The alfalfa patch greened with foliage, and Papa hired Charlie Ostrander from his homestead east in Cherry County to come and mow. It was from him that we acquired the Morgan stallion, Monte, formerly known as Monarch, of the Marcy herd. We planned to raise colts, not knowing that they would be too small to work and too big to handle cattle on sandhill trails. We piled the alfalfa in long ricks below the house, and soon we had the most hay we'd ever known. Mama's eyes gleamed, and Papa triumphantly showed off the alfalfa patches and haystacks to everyone that came. Our cows were well-fed that winter and produced a good calf crop.

We had learned a lesson about fuel the previous winter, and every nice day that fall, we were picking chips. Mama would go out in the afternoons and gather them in her big apron to make piles. Thirteen piles were considered a wagonload. Soon she had all the local ones together. Our herd did not furnish many chips, and the Spade steer chips were smaller and crumbly. It took cows in summer to produce platter-sized fuel, and these were mostly on the Margraves'. We ranged up to four miles, working around the windmills and lakes, gathering. We boys drove Brownie and Blackie, although they were expecting colts the next spring. Fritz went along to manage the team.

The spring rye Papa had planted in the South Valley produced a fine crop. Ostrander threshed it for us late, late in the season, and most of it was sold for seed to the neighbors, leaving a huge straw pile at the west end of the valley.

That fall we tried again to go to the Hebbert school. A settler had moved away with his children, and now there was room. We even furnished our share of the chips. But we were still unwanted extras, as we had been in the Peters school on the River. But it was considered un-neighborly to refuse to let us attend, as we had no school of our own. So we went, but they were probably looking for a chance to get rid of us. One day when I went to Lakeside to drive for Papa, the opportunity came. It seems Lulu Bixby, the teacher, suspected our brother James of throwing paper wads. She grabbed him out of his seat by his arm, and someway he tripped her, so she lost her footing and fell on her backside in the coal scuttle. The Drury kids laughed and shouted, and our family was expelled.

That fall, Papa made a wooden boat out of foot boards, and we used it to hunt ducks and trap muskrats in the Osborn and Jacobs swamps. We made coyote sets in the fireguards, caught only a few, but were more successful with strychnine.

In the spring he used that money to order another wagonload of trees. He and I drove to Lakeside to haul them out. We usually managed to stay with one of the Kicken families overnight, so Papa could get in some good French visiting. We now had our own four-horse team: Blackie, Brownie, Jennie, and Pacy. Next day after we got home, we took the family to the south valley. The smaller children played in the straw stack, while the rest of us planted the patch in mostly apple trees, and two rows of Omaha plums. There were no coon, robins, deer, nor antelope to hinder tree or fruit growth, and only tent caterpillars and curculios for insect pests. We replaced apple trees for those dead in the cherry orchard across the home valley, and now we had mixed cherry and apple trees all over the patch that later necessitated hunting all over for many years of fruit selling. Papa had not yet spent all of the winter's trapping money, so he ordered a hundred dollars' worth of peony roots. Mama wanted to know what he planned to do with the flowers if he raised any, but as so often, he chose not to hear.

After we were expelled from the Hebbert school for the second time, our father tried to organize a school district in February, 1912. He invited Cooks, Craigs, and people to the north to join. They did create a district and voted the schoolhouse four miles north to accommodate the Margraves. They built a schoolhouse of sod, and this became Spring Lake district. Papa gave up on that school and organized another one with the Strasburgers, Tuckers, Wests, Drbal, and Dukat. He included Marion Keyes, who had come with Albert Hill from Mitchell, South Dakota, to homestead here. Since he had been ordered out of the Dolly Varden Valley north three miles by the Margraves, he had located Keyes and Hill both in the Margraves' pastures.

This became District 163, the Sandoz school, to be held on our place. Now we needed a schoolhouse, but also a meeting place for the community. Mama wanted a hog barn and granary—she was tops at raising hogs—and I hoped for a horse barn. So a couple of loads of lumber were ordered and, as Mari wrote in *Old Jules*, nothing larger than a two-by-four and foot boards to build his famous Neuchatel-style barn 120 feet wide and 40 feet long, with a 20-foot-high gable, standing as the barns and houses our parent remembered from the old country. It was four feet from the ground to the eaves on the west end, with room for hogs, for cows, a room I immediately grabbed for the horses, a space rafter-high in the middle for hay, with an adjacent room that did double and triple duty over the years as schoolroom, bunkhouse, dance hall, meeting place, picture show room, and occasionally as an additional granary. It was a noble building, but I regretted we did not put the money into the Craig place, as he sold out owing us sixty dollars on a store bill. That would have helped us more than the barn, I thought.

That summer Mari and James again went to the Riverplace with the folks to stay to can and sell fruit. When the parents came home, Fritz was nine and Flora was six, so they could look after the store and hopefully see that Caroline came to no trouble. With Mama to help—she was feeling well again—the trees were not such an ordeal. But the alfalfa patches were now producing so heavily that even with the new barn, there was only room for a small part of the hay inside. We had no hay-sweeps nor jay-hawk stackers, so Papa again hired the whole community of settlers to help: the Squires family with Mabel, George, and three younger; the West family with Pearl and Olive; and the Tuckers with Lily and Hazel. Mrs. Tucker weighed three hundred pounds and was good force in pitching hay from the windrows onto the hayrack. Later in the summer when Mari came home as we were putting up the second cutting, she had to help fork the fragrant alfalfa back in the haymow. She felt very bitter about it, and never having done any heavy work, she found the haymow close and unbearably hot. She did not even enjoy the many pigeons flitting about as the hay filled up to the rafters, crowding their nests in the ammunition boxes, nests that contained squabs we expected to furnish meat for the household.

But Mama also did the cooking for twenty people. There were two tables full, and Flora and Pearl West sat at the sewing machine. Fritz was in charge of chores and kids, although Lily and Mabel were old enough to carry water and chips. Papa went hunting every day to get meat for the table, since he had no idea to pitch hay. That was work for "Grobians." But grouse and rabbits were so plentiful, it was only a matter of going out of sight of the house to get all he could carry.

Papa decided to institute a dance the last Saturday of every month, and in this way we could attract and keep up with the Pine Creek crowd. Uncle Emile's family sometimes came with a team and wagon in the afternoon and rested until dance time. Mari was fifteen by now and interested in the local cowboys. Emile's family was more interested in getting a man with a homestead and a few head of cattle. I was fascinated by all the girls, but too shy to do anything about it. The Davis boys, Clifford and Ruben, came to furnish music with their fiddle and portable organ folded up like a suitcase. But usually the music did not arrive before ten o'clock at night, and the crowd would sit around and try to entertain themselves with jokes, stunts, and visiting. The musicians milked their cows before starting from Pine Creek, and if the moon

was dark, it was slow going. There was an average of one
or two wire gates every mile, and that took time. But they
played until daylight, so everyone was satisfied. Usually
someone took up a collection at midnight for the music.
Mama furnished the home-cured ham sandwiches, and
the ladies brought cakes.

That fall Charlotte Wing from Pine Ridge came to
teach, and all of us but Caroline went to school, along
with Hazel and Lily Tucker and the West girls. The
teacher roomed with Mari in the ell, as she boarded with
us. We were nine at Mama's red-checkered tablecloth,
even without the usual guests that just happened by. Not
since Aunt Susie's stay on the Riverplace had we had a
young lady in the house. I was most interested in the
goings-on between the schoolma'am and the local young
men. I recall one bachelor neighbor calling on his white
horse, Snowball. Usually the teacher entertained him in
the schoolhouse, and this was fine, except that they
burned the next day's cow chips.

In order not to be out of place when things were
happening, our father taught us boys to play French
pinochle, and soon we had a game going every evening as
soon as the table was cleared, and often the teacher
joined. Papa could get very excited over a hundred-fifty
meld, four aces, or whatever, pounding on the table and
ruining the turn-up of the wick screw on the Rochester
lamp. Mama would be darning socks near the stove by
the dim light that filtered past the players. The little kids
played on the rug that Mrs. Beckler had given us in
payment of her homestead location.

Charlotte was Catholic, and Wray Macumber, Scotch-
Irish Protestant, came down to argue religion endlessly.

Charlotte was not as well-versed in geography as she could have been; we never could convince her that Austria and Australia were not the same place. But she knew enough to pass up the local swains and marry her boyfriend from South Dakota, Ed Hagel.

We were becoming almost self-sufficient with the store. About twice a year, Bill Sears would haul a load of flour for us from the Colclesser Mill on Pine Creek, and Raymond Kicken freighted groceries and hardware from Lakeside for retail. Papa still handled and reloaded shells. He had all the reloading tools necessary for rifle and shotgun shells. On some winter evenings when we needed a hot fire anyway, he would melt a small iron pot of lead on the cookstove. Mama complained because the high heat warped the stove top, and soon everything ran to one side of the frying pan, but this was of no moment. With a small iron dipper, the hot lead was poured into the molds, casting five at a time. We kids admired the shining bullets that fell from the mold, and after cooling, the smaller kids could line them up into corrals and fortresses. Some nights Papa would cast buckshot, but that was not so successful. The shot was not always round, and he laid a small board over them on the tabletop and rotated the board, attempting to even off the bulges.

Another night he'd bring out the reloading tools and lay them all out on the table. He'd screw the powder measure on the table edge and alert us boys to start handing him things. First he'd adjust the measure for the kind of shells, usually shotgun shells, for a gram or so of powder and then, taking six to eight casings in one hand, he'd work the small lever to put in just the right amount for each shell. One of us boys would take the shells and put in a wad, tamping it carefully in each shell. After the powder was added, the tool was changed to a shot dispenser. This time, a measure of shot was added, and another couple of wads tamped in. Next came the crimping. This had to be done carefully to ensure a tight fit all around. I remember one evening when he had shells, a hundred and fifty or more containing just the right amount of powder, setting open on the table ready for the first wad, his lighted pipe swiveled in his mouth and scattered live coals in several shells. This could have been a disaster with a small keg of powder setting open to one side and enough powder in the shells to blow up the house. Mama began to scream, but when Papa finally saw what was happening, he calmly stuck his fingers into the smoking shells and extinguished the coals by shutting off the air. Thus, he avoided an explosion.

Chapter IX

Gunpowder

As boys growing up, we were becoming adventurous. Even with Papa's mind ever busy to create work for everyone, the summer I was fifteen, James was fourteen, and Fritz was eleven, there were times when we goofed off. We tried making a bicycle using the shaft of the cornsheller. The shaft broke, and James threw it up on top of the flat-roofed house out of sight. We had a stabledoor shotgun, one of those that had a half-round steel cover to fit over the shell. It stood in a corner and had not been used for years. And then we had several kegs of powder: black smoke, smokeless, some of varying strengths and power. These kegs sat on shelves behind the store door above the vinegar barrel and were not to be disturbed except in the case of a lightning storm. Then the kegs were taken out in the bare yard and washtubs put over them for safety from explosions.

James wondered what would happen if we loaded a

shell in the stabledoor, poured the barrel full of several
kinds of gunpowder, and set it off. We decided to try that
by wiring the gun upright to a post across the yard east.
By fastening a long string to the trigger, we were ready
for action. We backed off across the yard to watch from
some safety, and I pulled the string. The gun exploded
with a satisfactory roar, the yard filled with blue smoke,
and when that cleared away, we found the gun, but the
stabledoor had disappeared forever. Too bad, for it would
be a fine relic now.

If we could not think of enough projects on our own,
we surely had neighbors that could help out. One Fourth
of July, Dick Wyant, who was sort of a general experi-
mentalist, came over to the store with his family, looking
for entertainment. Our folks were on the Riverplace. We
took Dick to the shop to look around. He saw our heavy
anvil with the one-and-a-half-inch hole that anvils seem
to be made with, and this gave him an idea. He had us get
some buckshot, and by pounding that together, he managed to plug the bottom of the hole. Together we lugged
that heavy piece out through the kitchen into the bare
yard. We sent Fritz after a foot of the fuse left from
blasting stumps on the river. Dick put in the fuse and
filled the hole with gunpowder, tamping it judiciously.
Then he cleared the yard of kids and, standing back,
lighted the fuse. The result was a disappointing thud that
raised the anvil only a few inches off the ground. Much
more satisfying were the tin cans and boxes that we blew
up later.

There was another time when we were home alone,
and our eyes strayed to Papa's assortment of guns resting

in their fan shape in the corner, by the store door. The stabledoor was gone, but there was another unusual shotgun that some settler had brought in. We decided to see how it worked, so we took it outside and braced it up against a post and, loading it, pulled the trigger. The kick was terrific and broke the heelplate. When our father came home and found the rubber heelplate in two pieces, he asked if anyone had shot the gun. We all said "no," because we really hadn't shot the gun, just fired it. He stuck his finger in the end of the barrel and brought it out black with powder soot, so he knew it had been fired. He grumbled for a week, and a licking would have been much preferable to the endless haranguing, but I guess we were getting too big for that.

Then there was the time we decided to shoot some snipes on a pond near the house. The gun we used was a heavy double-barrel and hard to shoot. James decided he'd have me rest the gun on his shoulder, and I would get the kick from the gunstock. But the gun kicked sideways and tore James' ear so it bled and bled. We had to go to the house and have Mama wash it off. There was another furor from our parents.

One of the few things we enjoyed doing with Papa was going fishing. Every spring most of the settlers would go on a camping trip to the big lakes about twenty miles east in Cherry County: Cottonwood, Pfiester, and King's Lakes. King's Lake was famous because it was rumored they had gambling devices at the local post office, but we never did see any. One spring we loaded the lumber wagon with fish nets, an eight-foot homemade boat, three empty vinegar barrels with the tops out, and a nice canvas tent with camping gear. Papa, James and I, along

with Albert Von Ruff—the latter Caroline's babysitter,
but formerly a souse from the Tabitha House in Lincoln,
who was sober enough when with us—hitched four
horses to the wagon and started towards the lakes. We
stopped at Vaughns' on the way, to visit and rest the
team. They had five or six girls, so it was an interesting
stop. It took all day to reach the lakes, but they were full
of carp and bullheads that were very good eating in the
spring.

The next morning, we strung the trammel net and
shook out the seine. We soon had several barrels of large
carp in water on the wagon. We spent the rest of the day
around the lake visiting with other campers and killing
time, so we could get an early start in the morning with
the fish cool in fresh water. We wanted to get home with
as many live ones as possible. This second night, the
weather turned cold, and we didn't have enough blankets
along. I curled up in my coat, since Papa took all the
blankets. Albert and James stayed up all night walking to
keep warm. When we reached home the next day, we
emptied the barrels into the forty-foot tank by the well.
The carp that floated were dead, and Mama butchered
and salted them right away. The live ones swam to the
deep end and were caught throughout the summer for
fresh fries.

We were learning with all these activities, and sometimes just watching the neighbors was entertaining. The
Spade cowboys would come to the store while looking
after their cattle in the valley west. I learned to watch for
them, because I really admired the way they could handle
cattle. They were probably the best cowboys that ever hit

the country. One especally, Norm Honea, could throw a big rope loop over a cow and, letting her jump part-way through, pull up the rope and catch her by both hind legs almost every time. This was done for doctoring and milking out. No Spade cowboy I ever knew tried to catch a cow by the head, because all she could do then was choke down.

But most of the summers we spent hoeing weeds out of the trees. Papa insisted that every one should be destroyed. Sometimes, instead of hoeing, I ran the walking plow with him cussing and shouting all the time. But when our team was too played out, Tucker or Barber or someone with fresh horses came to help. If anyone so much as scratched a tree, Papa would be raving for hours. But the care did pay off, and although we had to occasionally replace a tree, many lived and bore fruit, even by the third year.

Wray Macumber was becoming even more of a regular visitor in our home, staying for meals, entertaining us boys, arguing with Papa and the school teachers. Mari masked her interest in the sharp top-buggy with the red wheels and yellow trimming. She lived in her own world. We were not a close family, and few of us knew what the others were thinking. Our folks ruled us by competition, and we were shamed into conformity by comparison. So when she and James were left on the Riverplace the summer of 1913 to sell fruit, she rode Pacy to Rushville and took the teachers' examinations, although she knew it would be against Papa's wishes. Fortunately, she passed. This bolstered her courage, and when Mae Peters invited her to their wedding at the Sacred Heart Church, Mari was there. That fall Mari got the contract to teach our school, and since I was not about to go to school to someone smaller and competitive, I dropped out and helped Mama feed the cattle, gather chips, and dig the hundred bushels of potatoes we had raised. We put them in the open pit Papa had arranged in the cellar room. That winter, most of them froze, and Mama spent all her spare time sorting out the spoiled ones to feed the hogs.

But the hay in the barn was the biggest chore. The school kids were on it every recess, tramping until it was as solid as chewing tobacco. We had a hoe blade welded to a D spade handle and used that to cut the feed in pieces. It was almost impossible to do so.

I trapped several hundred muskrats, but no matter how much income we got, Papa spent it on guns, ammunition, credit to the settlers, and on stamps. I began to see that there were labor-saving devices that we should have, instead of just a pitchfork or its equivalent. Margraves used a jay-hawk stacker, a push sweep, and they could put up several stacks of hay a day, while it took us several days to put up a stack. Because we couldn't put up enough hay, we were out before spring and had to pull the straw stuffing out of the barn walls to feed to the cattle. Of course, they got poor, and we lost the "Whiskey Cow" we'd saved on the river and several others. The bulls had run wih the cows all the previous year, and the baby calves came in the freezing cold of January, took one breath, and died. When I suggested we lock the bulls away at certain seasons like the ranchers did, Papa cussed me out of the house. "Males should not be curbed," he roared. We got through the winter well enough, with Mari's salary to help.

When the school term was finished in 1914, Mari's teacher's permit was also expired. She could go to Teacher's Institute at Chadron to have it renewed, but for that she needed some of her wages. She and Papa had a big fight over that. He said she had not been eighteen, and the money was his. As usual, Mari bawled and carried on, and Mama paced around nervously. Meanwhile, Wray Macumber had proposed and had taken her to a dance or two at the neighbors'. Whether she saw it as a way out, or if she really thought she was in love, they went together to Rushville and got married. Our folks gave her a horse, a cow, featherbed, linen. It took a hayrack and four horses just to haul her things away, a dowry just as she would have had as a Swiss Miss.

They were soon completely absorbed by the Macumber family. Wray's mother was stylish, had been a milliner, wore large feathered hats, and was corseted like a fashion plate. She soon taught Mari not to look old country. That fall Mari taught the Strasburger school, riding Wray's horse Billie on a high run both ways of seven miles, so she would have time to feed the cattle before school and haul the coal in after school. She scarcely came home, seeming to prefer the Macumber family, their dinners, ballgames, and American ways. We boys missed Wray, and when we did see him, his whole attitude towards us had changed.

That fall, Ida Smith came to teach in our school. She was from Hay Springs. I went back to school, but had really lost interest in Papa's barn-school. The Wests had left the country, so there was only our family and Lily and

Hazel Tucker. That fall, a traveling photographer came
through and took pictures of us with Ida Smith as teacher.
Caroline got included in the pictures although she was
only four, not even registered in school yet, officially, or
even old enough to have her hair braided.

Ida enjoyed the dances and the still-bachelor Harry
Strasburger. By now, James was taller than I and more
conscious of girls. But I was more athletic. I could sit
cross-legged on the floor with folded arms and rise
straight up to a standing position. This didn't help me on
the dance floor, where even Fritz was beginning to spend
time. These dances held the teacher for the winter, and in
the spring, she left to marry her Hay Springs sweetheart,
a Mr. Duff.

On one of his trips to Alliance, Papa brought home an
orphan, Annie Shankman, about thirteen. She had been
around and knew a lot of things we'd never heard of
before. Mama saw this could not be tolerated with a
family of boys such as we were, and especially after we
took Annie along to a dance in the Drury house. It was an
unfinished homestead shack with no ceiling, but just
stringers above. Annie jumped and grabbed one of the
stringers. Swinging her legs back and forth, she kicked
the hat off Henry Case as he waltzed by, showing her
underwear—or lack of it. When Miss Tuttle came from
her homestead over southeast the next day, Mama sent
the girl home with that prim old maid. We heard that
Annie shocked Miss Tuttle with her gymnastics and was
returned to Alliance.

The living was getting easier. We had bought some

80 chickens from the Leggetts living in one of the two Margrave houses in the Jacobs valley. Another of the Craigs, living in the other, threw in a turkey gobbler. Mrs. Jim Cerny gave us three turkey hens, and we were in business to raise turkeys for years, until the coyotes got too thick.

When the folks went to the Riverplace the summer Mari married, they took Fritz in Mari's place along with James to sell fruit. Mari offered to keep Caroline for a week, and Flora and I were left alone. But about midweek when Flora went over to take fresh clothes, Caroline insisted on coming home and walked the mile and a half, although she was only four. Apparently she didn't like living with the Macumbers. So I had two little girls to look after.

One night a violent storm approached, and I carried the powder kegs out in the yard before going to bed. In the night, it began to hail and thunder and lightning. The boards on our flat roof were cheap lumber with lots of knots. As the hail continued, it shredded the rubber roofing and began to beat out the knots and come down on our heads. Water was gathering on the floor and soaking everything. I stood both girls on a dryer place and got a featherbed for them to hold over their heads, while we watched the storm. Next day and for several days, there was hail everywhere. Papa's hundred dollars' worth of peonies that had been blooming so beautifully were practically vanished, along with the leaves of the young trees, our alfalfa crop, and the corn in the north valley. When the folks came home three days later, you could look up through the roof and see the blue sky. Papa

sent to town for shingles and word to old Barber to come
and help. We shingled everything on the place. The barn roof worked fine, but the next rain flooded into the house, for there was only a three inch drop for every ten feet of roof. The house, excepting the store, leaked ever after.

Chapter X

Up At Uncle Bill's

Papa had made his final five-year proof on our Sandhills homestead, and the land was legally his and Mama's. But he never considered her interests. She was to do what he said, and that was that. One day I heard a ruckus in the house and ran down from the barn to look. Papa had Mama by the throat up against the wall, choking her. She was blue in the face and shaking, limp like a rag doll. I screamed as loud as I could that he was killing my Mama, and it got his attention. I thought he was going to come after me next, but he let go, and she crumpled to the floor in a heap. He went out the back door, and I got my mother back on her feet. I vowed that if I ever got big enough, I'd give him a threshing he'd never forget when he tried such a thing again, cripple or no cripple. I found out from the family that our father had been on one of his "damn the government" spells and wanted to sell the land and go to Canada. But Mama refused to sign the deed. I

think she figured he'd get the money, spend it, and we'd 83
be without anything again.

For some time after that, he avoided my eyes, and there
was no camaraderie between us. But friction had been
building up anyway. If Mama needed something done,
she no longer bothered consulting him. She'd have me
get the team, or do some riding after a cow, and he'd only
learn the details later, or not at all. Naturally, he resented
this.

Now I began to notice that my projects no longer
flourished. The two rows of cottonwood shoots I had
growing fine and shiny, began to look dull and listless.
Occasionally, one of my fish in the tank would be floating
dead on top of the water, for no apparent reason. Then
one day I saw Papa pull one of my cottonwood slips
loose, so I knew he was killing my trees and my fish. I
wanted to leave, but felt it was my duty to stay and help
out with the rest of the family, to see that Flora could
occasionally have some fun, that Caroline learned to
mind and observe other decencies. And that Fritz would
get a chance at a start, even to convincing James to give
him a share in the trapping.

But things were working to a climax. Papa had an
underground gasoline tank down the lane from the
house. Then when Prohibition came he decided to put in
an underground redwood tank to soak rye for hogs and,
incidently to make some alcohol for his evening hot
toddy. These underground tanks and the gasoline pump
above ground made it difficult to drive a team up and
down the narrow yard, especially since the loose sand
was inches deep. I began to agitate to widen the yard, but
this only served to stiffen my father's purpose, and he

planted a pear tree just north of the underground tanks. The pear tree grew and flourished, and as the branches spread, the yard got narrower. There were several incidents when Papa thought my team had touched his tree, but I was especially careful.

Then the third of July when I was sixteen, the pear tree leaves began to droop and show signs of dying. The next day, the Fourth of July, the tree definitely was in trouble. Papa got down on his hands and knees to examine the bark. He found the tree had been girdled with a sharp knife just under the ground level. No varmint could have done this; it was clearly man-made. Papa never thought to blame either of the other boys for anything. His mind always centered on me. Coming to the house in a towering rage, he ordered me out to the pear tree. I was amazed at the damage and could offer no excuse. He cussed and threatened and swore. He told me there was no longer anything on the place for me, to get out and not come back.

Mama had stayed in the background, and when I went to the barn, she came out with a few clothes bundled into a sack and told me I better go up to Uncle Bill's. No one saw me go nor heard from me for many months, but I'm sure she knew where I was and how I was doing. Uncle Bill and Aunt Lena made me welcome, and I was to help in or out of the house, and especially with Aunt Lena, since she had a crippled hip and could not get around well. They had no children of their own at home. Uncle Bill had a grown daughter, Esther, by a first wife who had died in Switzerland. Esther, now Mrs. Felix Sandoz, lived nearby with her family. They put me back in school to finish the eighth grade at Banner school. I met some of my friends from the Riverplace again: the Houshes, Sturgeons, the Great Uncle Paul Sandoz family, and the Peters boys.

This sojourn with Uncle Bill was one of the best things that could have happened to me. I learned how other people lived and worked. Uncle Bill and Aunt Lena were very good to me. In the first place, he was taking a very good chance that Papa would be furious at him for taking me in, and these two brothers had been very close. But, seemingly, there was no hesitation. Their home was far different than ours. Much of my time was spent with Aunt Lena and whatever concerned her. If she was house cleaning, so was I, and when dishes time came, she washed and I dried. She did not handle a team well, so if she wanted to go to town or to the neighbors and my uncle was not available, it was my job to take care of the team and drive and open gates.

While I never knew my parents to go visiting except to relatives on the river, this couple kept up a complicated social relationship that encompassed three distinct sets of friends that they visited back and forth with continually. They even at times managed to crack the social strata in Hay Springs, something that very few in the rural areas managed. Aunt Lena liked to visit in person and on the telephone. Those were party lines, and everyone knew everyone else's business. But while my father and Sturgeon were such good friends, I never knew the Sturgeons to visit in my Uncle's home.

I was expected to do good in school, and while we had so little schooling in the Sandhills, I thought I was holding my own. There were four in our class, and when the eighth-grade examination results came in, one of the neighbors called to tell my aunt that all had passed but me. My aunt was angry, and it was a very unjust thing for this neighbor to have done, for I had passed. And I was the only one of the three boys in my family to get an eighth-grade diploma.

Uncle Bill raised bees and sold honey. He had always brought several supers of combs and whole hives to our home in the hills on his annual visits, but we were never bee-minded and could not manage the hives. I was no better up there, but I could milk cows, run a separator, handle horses, even if my weight was only 98 pounds and my build slight. But under the different environment, I began to grow.

Not long after I got to Uncle Bill's, I went riding with Jack Anghern, a nephew of Uncle Charlie Grossenbacher, Felix Sandoz, and Steve Peters. We decided to go swimming in a deep hole in the Niobrara. I was in a playful mood, and when Jack took his shirt off, I threw it out in the river. Jack was furious and, grabbing me, threw me into the deep water. He fished out his shirt and, with the others, got on their horses and rode away. I don't know how I got out; I couldn't swim, had never learned even though they'd put me on a sandbar when I was five or six and tried to make me wade or swim ashore. But I woke up lying on the bank with my lungs full of water.

The Felix Sandoz family lived not far away, and the two families visited and worked back and forth constantly. Esther drove one horse on a box cart carrying the children, Clarence, Allie, and Blanche. She had been

raised by Grandmother Sandoz in Switzerland, and they
all talked French fluently.

I was thankful now for my training by Mrs. Surber. I could get by in this household where the niceties of living were observed. I could say "please" and "thank you" and hold the door for a lady. But after about a year, I began to notice little frictions developing. For one thing, Uncle Charlie let it be known that I should have come to them because Mama's family was Aunt Susie's only relation in this country. The neighbors remarked that Uncle Bill should be paying me wages since I was out of school and helping do the farming. And he did pay me some, and I had sent Papa a check for 25 dollars for the horse I had ridden away. Too, the grandsons, Clarence and Allie, were growing up and could help Aunt Lena, so I wasn't so much needed there. It reached a head one day when I was sent to look after the geese setting on eggs. We had never had geese, and I knew nothing about them, especially that they take much longer to hatch than chicken eggs. I'd marked down the date of the setting, and when 24 days had passed and nothing had hatched, as would have with chickens, I broke the nests up and threw the eggs out. It was a stupid thing to do. Maybe Bill was in a bad mood, too; anyway, when he found the eggs thrown away and cold, he said I should go and take a regular job someplace else. He would rent the farm land to the Peters boys and help Lena himself.

It was only a short way to the Elmer Sturgeon farm and holdings, and there was always lots of work there. I moved over there, and in that place, I could really be grateful to Mrs. Surber. Sturgeon was polite in everything. He neither drank nor swore, and his wife, the former Emma Bray, did not work outside as Mama had done. Professor Sheldon wrote in his *Geography of Nebraska* that Sturgeon was the foremost breeder of Percheron horses in America, and Hay Springs was famous for its many fine imported stock.

Sturgeon had two hired men, Art Basil and a man named Poague. Most of my work was to help care for those fine horses. There was a huge barn that stabled forty head on each side, eighty head of horses that had to be led out and watered, fed, their stalls cleaned, their coats curried, their manes and tails tied or braided. Here I met again the imported mares, Mimi and Mollie, that Pearl and Olive West had ridden around the Sandhills. There was a special box stall for the imported stallion, and he had to be exercised daily. Usually Sturgeon did this himself, driving the animal everywhere hitched to a one-horse buggy. If Mrs. Sturgeon wanted a team to go to town, Poague or I would get the rig ready. She was an accomplished horsewoman and, while she occasionally had a runaway, she could and did drive to Hay Springs every week by herself.

Sturgeon raised a lot of potatoes, and that winter on days that were above freezing, I would freight spuds to town to be shipped out on the railroad. We had to be careful with the horses, and I was trusted with the prize team of Beauty and Lady Milton. I remember driving across Walgren Lake when the dust blew up in clouds. There was no monster there then.

Some days we were dynamiting the stumps along the

Niobrara near the Sturgeon bridge. I remembered our
experiences with explosives on the river and at home, and
I knew it was dangerous. We were using forty-five power
sticks. Poague, who was older and had been at Sturgeon's
longer, was the leader. But he was sort of a reckless cuss.
We would load a box of the red sticks in an open wagon
and start for the river. We had to be careful not to make
the horses sweat, but Poague would urge them into a
gentle trot anyway. I imagined every minute that those
dynamite sticks would go off as I sat in the back of the
wagon with my legs hanging out. But they never did.

After dynamiting stumps out, there was about a three-
foot hole left, which I filed with gravel from the river. We
planted a tree in each of these and filed it partly with
water. The Mirage Flats soil was so impervious to water
that if the holes were filled, the trees would have drowned
before the excess seeped away or evaporated.

When it turned realy cold, we cut ice for a month to fill
the ice house on the farm. Nearly everyone of substance
did this. The ice was cut with saws into two-foot chunks
and hauled up from the river, packed in a lot of straw,
where it would last probably until August. When we
were through with that, Claud Sheffner and Ed Zink
came over, and we sawed a long strip of ice to set a
trammel net. We worked all day and caught one fish.

Sturgeon had land in the Sandhills south of the river,
and in summer I rode down there once a week to look
after the cattle and the water. I passed in sight of the Todd
and Ebough race track, which was close to the Ault and
Skudlas places. Todd and Ebough were gone, but I could
still make out the race course.

There was a nice lot of social life around, and since

everyone had a big barn, many of them gave dances when the barns were empty. Even Great Uncle Paul, two miles away, who didn't dance or favor it, gave a dance in the new barn he built. Pochons gave an annual dance until lightning burned the barn down. The Emile Sandoz children gave a dance in their barn, although it was much smaller. And always, there was horse racing.

Other than feeding and watering the horses, we were free on Sundays and could ride any of the off-colored horses that were not suitable to sell to the Army Remount Station at Fort Robinson. So I took to riding around the community to see friends. It was while at Sturgeons I had my first date. I rode to Palmer's Grove down the Niobrara to a Fourth of July celebration with Cecile Dykes. We had known the Dykes family for years, and her brothers were my friends, so it was more of a friendly ride than a date. It was at that dance that George Hare and Mrs. Tom Tallon won first prize for a waltz. On the way home, one of the men driving Sturgeon's buggy team ran a race with Johnny O'Mara and Constance Sandoz. On turning in at DePorter's bridge, the buggy upset. But no damage was done. The buggy was uprighted, the team brushed off, and we went on.

One day that summer, we were fixing fence on the Niobrara when a storm came up. Even in the deep valley of the river, we could see the clouds boiling and churning. We drove home as fast as possible and met Mrs. Sturgeon at the door. Her husband had called from Hay Springs to tell everyone to go to the ice house, from which we watched the tornado. We could see the progress of the storm as there was no hail or rain, just tumbling

wind. Fences, buildings, sheep, and debris were sucked
up into a funnel in the sky. At the O'Maras' neighboring
sheep ranch, the storm rolled up a huge ball of woven
wire, posts, sheep, trees, gates, and brush. The ball came
out of the top of the funnel and fell to the ground. That
pile was more than an acre across and lasted for many
years as a landmark.

The work slacked off at Sturgeon's, and I decided to
look for another job. I'd traded my horse from home to
Mrs. Poague for doing my laundry. So I bought a black
riding pony, one that pleased me very much. I just started
riding acoss the Flats asking here and there for work. The
banker, Magowan, had a feed yard, so I settled there.
Other young men were working there, and since it was
very close to town, several of us young men would ride in
to the barn dance hall called the Chicken Roost. World
War I had started, and the Bohemians and the Germans
were very bitter towards one another. Before the nights
would be over, they would have several fights. I never
took part, but enjoyed watching from a distance as they
threw one another out of the big hay mow door.

The work at the yards was of various kinds, and in
spring they put me in the cellar cutting potato seed with
one of the Parchen girls. After a whole day of sitting
down there and that girl never saying one word to me, I
decided to move on. Magowan was not at home when I
left, so the foreman, Shubert, gave me an interest-bearing
note, and the bank cosigned for it. Work became hard to
find, and I headed my horse south into the Sandhills to
see what I could find there. I had a little money besides the
note, so I felt confident. When I couldn't get a ranch job

under the Sandoz name—Papa was still bitterly opposed—I would go by the name of Jules Alexander. They would be more interested, but I still didn't get a job. I drifted into Alliance and stabled my horse on the edge of town.

I went to a rooming house, and they put me in a room with an older man. We had never needed to fear anyone, and I was very green. However, when this older man began to watch me undress, I got nervous and remembered what Sam Speer had told Papa about the men in Alaska. I buttoned my clothes back up and told my roommate I was going out for a sandwich. He followed me out, and when I got free, I began to run. He tried to catch me, and as we ran around Alliance, I was glad I knew the town and could lose him for awhile. But I was really scared now and decided I'd better not go back to the hotel. I was familiar with the Burlington yards and went down and got on a freight train. Before I got to Sidney, he found me, and I thought maybe I could give him the slip by jumping off and starting to run again. He was right behind me, when I heard a dog bark. I thought the dog was a better bet, so I ran around a big evergreen bush in a Sidney backyard. The dog held the man off, so I could get back to the train and board again for Denver. However, the man made it to the train, too. In Denver, I tried again to give him the slip in the railroad yard by crawling up into an empty coal car. I made it, but there was about six inches of snow and ice water in the bottom. I about froze before making it back to Sidney, where I was glad to buy a ticket to Alliance and ride inside. When I got back to the rooming house next day, I told the manager about my experiences. He explained to me about sex deviates and inexperienced boys and the danger I'd been in.

I realized I'd seen about as much as I wanted to for one hitch, so next day decided to ride for home and see how things were. Also, I'd had a notice from the draft board to register. Everyone at home seemed glad to see me, and the only aftermath was when papa would get mad at me, he'd remind me I'd cheated him out of two years' work. I'd grown to almost six feet and filled out considerably. For the first few weeks, my father paraded me in front of all and bragged inordinately about "his son." Of course, that was short-lived, and fortunately so, for I found his bragging harder to bear than his criticism.

Chapter XI

The Tucker Place

One of the first things I did on arriving home was to move us boys out of Papa's room into the schoolroom in the barn. It was no longer needed for that purpose. The district had hired Joe Drbal, who was a carpenter, to build a new schoolhouse a mile and a quarter west to accommodate the Hooley family, who had moved in as neighbors to Wray Maccumber. We had a stove out there in the barn, so it was a small matter of carrying our beds and bedding to the barn. Papa'd quit giving dances because of the vandalism and thievery that went on and had divided the room in half. So it was easy enough to take the Canadian maps of the Peace River, where he'd planned to go at one time, and paper the walls and ceiling. We built a table of foot boards, and with more boards on top of some empty vinegar barrels, we were set up.

We began trapping muskrats in November, but it was harder to manage. Furs had increased in value six and

seven times since the World War, and Russian furs quit
coming on the market. The owners of lakes sent the hired
help to run off anyone trying to trap. Papa could not
accustom himself to this; trapping had always been free
and should always be so. But I could see we boys would
have nothing to do all winter without trapping, so I made
a deal with the Margraves for half and ordered three
hundred steel Newhouse traps. Our father continued to
set the small lake we had east of our house and on our part
of the Alkali Lake in the Osborn Valley. He took those
rats to the house and hung them behind the stove to dry.
Mama helped him to skin and stretch them later.

We boys drove shingle nails in rows along the bunk-
house walls, and when we came home from trapping, cut
slits in the tails of each animal and hung it up to dry. After
supper, we skinned the muskrats, scraped the fat from the
hides, and stretched them on wire frames or nailed them
on shaped boards made from the wooden packing cases
that came with store goods. We threw the carcasses up on
the barn roof to dry for dog feed in the summer. We
would get fifty and sixty rats a day, often some mink, and
a few skunks from dens here and there. Fritz amused
himself catching ermine.

I was nineteen now, and the money seemed to be
rolling in. One of my brothers and I would feed Mama's
cattle, haul some hay in the corral for the milk cows, and
for the saddle horses that were a necessity with trapping
several miles away in the Jacobs, Goose Lake, Smith
Lake, and Willow Valleys. I was happy that winter, as
never before. Every day I could see that long Willow
Valley four miles north on the Margraves and think how

it could be drained and become dotted with haystacks and cattle.

Coyotes were becoming plentiful, and with all the muskrat carcasses, it was inevitable that we would acquire more hounds. First we had some give-aways from Hoppes and Short. But we soon learned that dogs varied even more than people. I began to watch carefully for bloodlines and training. For this I needed some way to keep a record, and I spent some of my first money from furs on a good folding Kodak. The camera proved a godsend in preserving records of not only the hounds, but of the big barn, the old house, the trees, corrals, horses, and how everything looked at the time. Some of the pictures in my sister's book *Old Jules* came from this camera.

All this time, we were subscribing to the *Hunter, Trader, Trapper,* a well-established magazine of the time. It carried many ads for dogs and was the vehicle for Papa's strychnine trade. I soon was exchanging pictures and ads of hounds. At the time, Ben Ammon of Bassett was the leading hound man of Nebraska, so I bought several from him. They would be shipped in crates on the railroad, and we would have to try to get the mail really often in order to get shipping notices on time. Station agents had no dog food, nor any desire to care for live animals. These dogs were mostly greyhounds, lean and fast. But I thought we needed heavier dogs; the greyhounds were catching the coyotes, but usually were outfought. So James and I bought two big hounds, Buck and Blue, from Minnesota. They weighed about a hundred pounds each and stood three feet tall. Then we needed hounds that could track a scent, so ordered a bloodhound from Missouri.

But he was too slow and noisy, and spent his time trailing every skunk, rabbit, and tabby cat. So we crossed that into the mixture we were raising. All the time, we were trading locally, even boarding out hounds for the summer when they overran the home place. The *Trapper* bragged on the beagle, so we tried that, too. It was trained for coons, and at that time, we had no coon in the country. Other than a melodic bark, that one did us little good. Later, we had a white dog that was part wolf and never really became tame or trustworthy.

Gradually we evolved several superior packs, usually three to five dogs, that we ran perhaps once or twice a week, alternately. We rode the saddle horses the same, because it took a lot of riding to locate the game. Soon we knew most of the individual coyotes by sight, and it was a challenge to get the last ones, which we never did, since in February the coyotes and dogs go into breeding season and no longer will fight one another.

I was keeping all of my share of the money we made, and James and Fritz were never asked to share theirs, but World War I was heating up and the draft board becoming insistent. Just when I was approaching my twentieth birthday, the Armistice was signed, and everything was declared on hold. Prices went higher than ever. We stepped up our hunting and trapping all around. With hounds from Ben Ammon, from Price Hobbs, who had 31 dogs on his place west of Gordon, and some Russian and Irish wolfhounds from here and there, we caught coyotes almost every time we went out, over 150 that winter.

But there were accidents. Once when James was out

with one of our broncs, a bitch, Little Blue, got too close to the hind hooves and the pony kicked, crushing the dog's head. James forlornly led the horse home, leaving Little Blue lying by the north gate. I went over to take a look—that hound was the core of one of our best packs—and saw that she was still alive. I carried her home in my arms, and in a couple of weeks she was quite a bit better. The next season, she ran with the best.

The loss of a good dog could seriously hamper our coyote kill, and the next Fourth of July when I locked up the hounds to accompany Mama, Flora, and Caroline to a celebration at Bean Soup Lake, the dogs got in a free-for-all and killed my best hound. I was so mad, I took a neckyoke and killed the trouble-maker, which I should have done before, excepting that he was a good dog, too. People were raising dogs for us for $35 each, summering them for $10, but a really well-trained dog could bring over $200. But the loss of those two dogs the Fourth broke up our packs, and they never again reached their finest ability.

But there was constant friction with Mama and the girls about the hounds. The dogs ate everything on the place: the turkey eggs, the chicken eggs, they got on the salted meat, and, since we had no screens on the house, they stood packed in the kitchen door at mealtimes, slavering and edging ever closer to the table. Caroline was so upset that they chased her pet cat, until finally the grey and white tabby disappeared completely. And we used her saddle horse to chase coyotes. In fact, to keep in enough good fast horses, we traded continually with the grubliners, Andy Brown, Charlie Sears, Gene Sutton, and Pat Snyder, to get rested ponies. One day in an

enthusiasm of trading, I swapped off Caroline's favorite
pony. While it was hers in name only, nor even mine
exactly, I had to give her a much better horse, Blackie,
that she remained glued to for years, so much so that I
couldn't even raise colts with the mare.

When I came back from Uncle Bill's, James was already giving the local girls quite a chase. I decided I
should do this, too. A box supper was scheduled at the
Strasburger schoolhouse, and the whole community attended. I never was one to throw my money around, and
when the boxes came up for bids, I watched who was
bidding and how much. Too, in those days, we watched
whose cooking we were getting. There were women in
the community whose cooking our Sandoz family considered unsafe because of copper cooking kettles and
ignorance of chemical reactions. But we all knew that
Mrs. Beckler was a good, clean, knowledgeable person,
and she'd had a gathering of some local girls at her house
to fix boxes. Among them was Gladyce, an orphan thirteen-year-old girl, Ruth Crofutt, and a local school
teacher from the Spade district. We could safely bid on
those. Carl Mills, who hung around the Spade ranch,
was bidding on what he thought was the teacher's box.
He was going by the crepe paper used, the style of the
box and the way it was made. But there were two boxes
especially alike. I thought one was Gladyce's, a friend of
Caroline and often around our place, so I bid on it. Carl
thought I knew something he didn't, so he ran it up to
five dollars. That was too much money for me, so I let
him have it and bid on the similar box. Well, he had to eat
with the thirteen-year-old, who was considered just a

child in those days, and I ate with the teacher. It was one of my few triumphs, but just a little off-flavor, for I was sure the schoolma'am would rather have eaten with Mills. I still hadn't learned to do all the little things like hold a girl's hand a bit long, get one last squeeze in a dance, or give an especially accented "thank you," like Carl and James could do.

In spring, the Pochons came from Pine Creek to visit. The mother, Eugenie, sister of Uncle Bill's Lena; her son Roger; and daughters Henriette and Emma came in a big new Reo touring car to spend the night and take home a bushel or two of asparagus from Papa's two-acre patch. Henriette and Emma were dazzling in their big feathered and flowered hats, and much more mature than my nineteen or twenty years. The young ladies would stay with Eugenie to visit Mama and Papa, while Roger would take us boys and Flora and Caroline to get the mail at the Spade post office about seven miles away at the Henry Case place.

One time after the Pochons left, Papa decided to buy a car, too, so we could get the mail so handily, and go fishing. Of course, we couldn't afford a new Reo. He bought a second- or third-hand Model T that was a real lemon. He also ordered a heavy iron-wheeled trailer from Montgomery Ward on which to load a boat. When the trailer came, we loaded the wooden boat, with James at the wheel of the Ford. I was never allowed to drive that car. We menfolks took out one morning for the lakes. The Ford soon got hot, and we unloaded the trailer, unhitched the boat, and pulled it the rest of the way by a rope over the sand. On coming home, the car gave out completely, so I borrowed a horse from a settler to get our team and pull the outfit home.

The year before I got home from the Mirage Flats, the folks bought the Tucker place. That Oklahoman got the moving yen and delivered an ultimatum. Either we bought his place, or he'd sell to someone else. Well, we couldn't spare James and Fritz anymore to go to the Riverplace to sell fruit, so we sold that place to the one-armed Swiener. Besides, the orchards in the Sandhills were beginning to bear and furnish a great deal of fruit.

Papa didn't get around much anymore, so Mama and I discussed what we should do with the Tucker land. That former neighbor had not raised much because he didn't have any machinery. He would scatter alfalfa seed by hand on plowed ground and have his daughter Lily drag a mower wheel around to cover by horseback. But I had farmed for Uncle Bill and Sturgeon and knew how it should be done and what we needed. I bought a single-row lister from Uncle Bill for forty dollars and ordered a go-devil from the catalog. Uncle Bill had bought a two-row lister, since he had bigger horses. The twelve-hundred-pound Morgan cross, Buster, was the biggest one we had, so single-row was our best bet. Even then, it took four horses. In May, I hitched up and drove to the Tucker field and listed from the Spade ranch school section line to the Big Tucker Hill, planting bushels of yellow seed corn. Then I plowed Papa's trees and went back to run the go-devil I brought out from Lakeside. I recall we'd stopped at Joe Or'Kuskie's to stay the night. In the morning, Mrs. Or'Kuskie came out to look at our freight load. She was Bohemian and not too sure of her

English, so she asked me, "What are you going to do with the 'go-to-hell'?" James and Fritz had been spending their summers on the Riverplace selling fruit, and since that was not exactly challenging, it probably was harder for them to visualize what could be done. They didn't exactly know what the go-devil was for, either.

That summer, we were helping Barber thresh, eleven miles east. He had gotten Worena, with his little gasoline engine that threshed very slowly. It would take several days, and the men all hated to help because he had no women and was not exactly a competent cook, although he told Mama one time that he could make better pot pie than any woman he knew. When evening came, there was no place to sleep, except in the rye bin, nor were there any blankets. We wondered why he didn't let some of us have his bed, which was customary when neighbors helped without being paid. Years later, we found out that he had the gun sewed in his bed, the one he'd shot the Ostrander cattle with when they got in his corn. Of course, he couldn't let anyone find that out. That same night, our horse Buster got loose and wandered over to the threshing machine and overate on waste rye. He got foundered and, though he limped the rest of his life, he still was always a dependable horse. Barber always had good horses, and it was on that trip when I traded Barber out of a fine saddle horse, Johnny, a five-gaited pacer, that I always loved to ride, and James hated with a passion.

One year when Barber was at our place threshing, and Wray Macumber was there, too, they got in a fist fight over the German war, but really over Mari. Mama actually pushed them out the back door; she'd have no fist fights in her house. When Barber died years later, he'd willed everything he had to Mari; she still had the will, but by then he'd nothing left. The lawsuit with the Ostranders had cost him his place.

Sugar and sweets were rationed during the war, so Papa had me plant sugar cane in the North Valley. We raised a bumper crop, and James and Fritz stripped some and hauled it home. They cut and piled the rest for the cattle. Papa took the rubber wringer of Mama's washer apart and put in iron pipes for rolers. We rolled out a couple of wash boilers of juice, and Mama cooked it down into the sorghum she'd seen in Arkansas at her Uncle Conrad Fehr's. The sweetener was successful enough, but she had to wring the clothes by hand for years until another rubber-rollered wringer could be bought.

The corn crop on the Tucker place produced big ears and lots of them. We hired Andy Brown to start husking. This was something Andy liked to do. He could do it alone and at his own pace, out at daybreak and work till sundown. Usually he had such a load in the evening, he'd have to go around our South Hill through John Strasburger's yard, and it would be late into the night before he reached home. Often Mama would phone the Strasburger ladies to see if he had gone through there yet, for one never knew if Andy was still on the job. Earlier, Andy had helped Papa build a big corn-crib bordering the yard on the west side (and the following year, another on the east side). There could no longer be any consideration of widening the yard. But I'd learned to accept a lot of things at Sturgeon's and Uncle Bill's, so nothing was said. I'd learned to accustom myself to the inevitable.

Tucker had been so anxious to leave, he threw in a whole bunch of tools, some posthole diggers, the pump organ, a free-standing wardrobe, and some other furniture. And with it all, we got a whole set of buildings to tear down. This really was a challenge. He had nailed the two-by-fours and timbers of his tin dairy barn with the five-inch notched nails that were almost impossible to pull. We would tear down the barn in pieces small enough to haul home and lay them out in the yard where the family could spend their spare time pulling nails. It was from this lumber that Fritz and Papa built a garage for the Model T that wouldn't run, and set it inside on blocks for a couple of years, where the kids played "car." Something broke the windshield, but even then Papa was able to sell it for $125, which is what he'd paid for it. Mama promptly moved her chickens into the garage, and for the first time in memory we had a real chicken coop.

Just as the snakebite turned out to be a blessing by getting us off a dry place and onto hay land, this buying of the Tucker land was the turning point in our ranching. I built a big tin corral connecting the barn to the new well and tank. The old Dempster mill had worn out and the forty-foot tank filled with sand. The windmill screeched on for another five years without oil, and the tank blew full of sand and was abandoned, although for ten years we'd dug it out every spring.

On Sundays in summer, the local young men and boys gathered at our place, and we began breaking the descendants of the old Fox mare. If we could get them broke

enough to trade to the local star boarders, they soon
became tame and gaunted down to almost a skeleton. The
Humane Society did not get as far as the Sandhills in those
days. Some of the broncs were adamant to the end, and
broke their necks lunging at the ropes, rather than take a
bridle and saddle. James was probably the best rider for
show, and Fritz did well after he got a formfit cantle. But
with my long legs, I could have doubled for Abraham
Lincoln. It took quite a horse to unwind me once I got set.
But I never learned to scratch with the spurs, as was
necessary for rodeos.

One day in late summer, 1919, Wray Macumber came
down to our place in his Model T touring car. He was
crying when he told Mama that Mari had left him and got
a divorce. We had not seen them for some time, and surely
Mari never said anything to any of our family that she
was unhappy. In fact, the last real contact we'd had with
them was 1917 when Papa went with the Macumber
family to Lincoln. Mari and a lot of others from Sheridan
County went there on a booster trip. There is a picture in
the Sheridan County Historical Society showing all those
who went. Papa said Wray swore at my sister at every
gate because she didn't seem to be opening and shutting
them as fast as he'd liked. But most men we knew swore
at their wives, so that was not considered unusual.

Wray said Mari had come in on the 27th of August and
announced she wanted a divorce. She wanted nothing of
their land or cattle, just $1200 in government bonds that
she had earned teaching. Wray agreed to that, and they
went to Rushville. There the District Court granted a
decree of extreme cruelty by the defendant and said the

plaintiff, Mari Sandoz, was entitled to an absolute divorce. Mama was terribly upset. She had never considered that way out of her own marital troubles and could not understand a daughter bringing such disgrace on the family. She always quoted Sophie Sears as saying, "When you burn your hindside, you sit on it."

We heard by the grapevine that Mari had gone to Uncle Emile's family and was teaching the Pine Creek school, with Rosalie Sandoz as one of her pupils. When the director, Ofzarzak, came to the schoolhouse one day to discuss our sister's teaching methods, she quit in a huff and went to Lincoln with Rosalie and enrolled in the Lincoln School of Commerce. Mari probably remembered her way around that city from the booster trip.

Anyway, Wray now had her trunk in the back seat of the car, and when he brought it in, he said that her stamp collection and $1200 in bonds was inside. We had no key, and years later when Mari wanted her bonds and sent the key, there was no stamp collection inside. Anyway, it had taken four horses and a hayrack to move her away, but her belongings had come back in a trunk.

That winter, James and I rented the three Margrave ranch lakes for cash. Earl Margrave counted the muskrat houses and decided he wanted two thousand dollars— seven hundred in cash and the rest in corn. We set up a bachelor's camp in the old Heywood house by Billy's Lake, northeast of my favorite Willow Valley. We took Fritz in for an equal share, although he had no money to put in, then hired Lawrence Macumber, Gene Sutton, and Charles Sears to help. We bought groceries in town, since Papa did not stock what we needed: puffed rice,

puffed wheat, cornflakes, cold meats, and baker's bread.
We borrowed cooking utensils, bedding, and all the spare
horses from home. Since we could not be around to look
after the cattle, Papa hired Frank Wildman, a late settler
from New York, to feed and trap the small lakes around.
Frank brought his own saddle horse, since Caroline was
still riding Blackie to school.

Our success at trapping discouraged other trappers,
and I was able to sublease from Scott Taylor a lake he had
on half share from Margraves. I was to get half of his half,
or a fourth. He'd been getting about seven rats a day. The
first day I went up there, seven miles, he traded me a
horse for $25. He'd not had breakfast yet. I went out and
set traps, and by noon had enough hides from my fourth
to pay for the horse.

It was an exciting winter, and once when we had a
bunch of hides, Earl Margrave and I took fourteen hundred skins to Gordon on a sled. The offer we got in
Gordon was unsatisfactory, so I called up the Strange
Brothers' Fur Company in Sioux City, Iowa. They
bought the furs sight unseen for double the price offered
locally. Papa had been selling to them for years, and they
knew the Sandoz name and the quality of furs we offered.

Fritz was absent many times on trips down to see
Frances Macumber about four miles away, and James was
gone every weekend to see Marie Dukat in another direc-
tion. It was a job to keep everyone trapping and cooking.
We still took our washing home to Mama to do on the
washboard. Gene Sutton would get drunk and think he
was riding a bronc as he scratched away on a round-
topped trunk, sometimes managing to get down in the

trunk, so we'd have to haul him out to keep him from choking. Charles Sears got in a hassle with Kenneth Fish and Frank Hoyt, who were working for Margrave. James and I had to rescue them. We had a continual game of poker going all winter, and in the spring Lawrence Macumber, I think it was, had $1.92 to the good.

Chapter XII

Farming for Myself

That summer, I rented the George Macumber place for seven hundred dollars in advance. It was some four miles south in Survey Valley and had a nice flat of farm ground. Dave Dexters had been living there after they traded their chophill homestead in Modisett's pasture to Earl Margrave for an old Model T touring car. Then I took in 150 of Mrs. Beckler's cattle for three dollars a head for the summer. James and I also rented farm land from the Strasburgers, particularly Emma Strasburger Merrihew, and some land in the Osborn Valley from old Ed Strasburger. I arranged to do the farming for our family on the Tucker place for the loan of some horses, and headquarters.

With all this land to farm, we'd have to have more horses. James bought a team of shires from Pete Anderson, big, slow, dependable horses, but nothing to handle quick broncs with. I found a pair of prospective unbroken workers from the Kickens, along with some others less promising. I was to break them for the summer's use. These horses had run loose all their lives, some seven, eight, and nine years old, mostly blacks, and tough. Not halter-broken or anything, but big. I got some other wild ones from Art Russell and a few unbroken ones from our folks. In all, we had 21 head, plus two broke teams from home. It was too late to tame them before corn-planting; the best we could do was take them on the swing side of a freighting team to town. But we found just corraling them a job.

I set up housekeeping in the Macumber house where Mari and Wray used to visit his family. His mother and father were divorced; she went to Missouri to live with a daughter, Esther, and George went to Chadron, where he had a twin brother. Fritz was helping me most of the time, and it would take a half day to get a four-horse team hitched and ready to work. We grabbed a sandwich and worked till dark, forcing the team onward in order to be able to handle them. By the time the corn was planted, most of them were scarred and gaunted, but still fighting. It was an effort to keep going. But we lost only one horse, and that was one of Papa's of Fox descent; she cut her side badly while tied to a steel windmill tower and had to be destroyed.

We cultivated the corn twice, and with lots of rain, a bumper crop grew. The next struggle was to get it shucked. I hired everyone available, and they came and went. Archie Kime stayed the longest. There was a Mr. and Mrs. Miller, but they were so dirty. Their little dog died in their bed, and it was a week before she made the bed and found it. Then Arthur Tucker, who had sold us his land, came with his daughter Hazel. He had worked his way back from Missouri to run a hotel in Clinton. We all liked Hazel. She was one of Caroline's friends, but more grown up. Everything was cheap now, especially corn, so instead of buying and hauling coal, Hazel, who was doing the cooking, burned corn. Mama said it was a sin to burn food, and that I'd never again raise a corn crop like that. And I never did. Cattle were cheap, too; steers were fifteen dollars a head. John Sears had mortgaged their homestead to Modisett to pay for a Majestic range; they never could pay the loan off, so Modisett got their homestead for a stove.

All fall I hauled corn at 45 cents a bushel delivered to the Margraves, as I'd agreed in the trapping deal. I had raised seven thousand bushels without irrigation. I bought pigs and raised hogs until I had a couple of hundred head. Of course, there was no way to keep them from going down to the neighbors who lived just east of the field, and soon I had quite a few dead hogs.

We had done so well on the trapping the winter before that the Margraves decided not to let us have it again. So we seeded all of the corn ground into rye, 300 acres. The next July, Fritz started running the binder, and Flora began shocking the bundles right behind. She wanted money for high school and kept up the whole way, all 300 acres. When we started threshing in the fall, I had my own machine. I had Johnny Myers and Gene Sutton working for me. One Saturday, this help wanted to go to a dance at the Downings east some 25 miles. I felt we had to keep threshing in order to get done before winter. The help felt differently, and about the middle of the afternoon, a 26-inch monkey wrench went through the separator of the threshing machine and broke it down completely. They went to the dance, and in the morning, Johnny told me it was too bad I'd not gone to the dance. Rosie Kirchner was there, and he had eaten supper with her. "Sure a nice girl you got there, Jules."

That winter of 1922 and 1923, Mari came home at Christmas-time. When she and Rosalie had gone to Lincoln in 1919, they continued with the Lincoln School of Commerce for nine months, until they ran out of money, and then took jobs. Mari went to Osceola to work in a county agent's office for two weeks. She decided the business world was not for her, so she went to the University of Nebraska and renewed her teaching certificate.

There was a vacancy in Cheyenne County near Sidney, so she moved there and boarded with the Pat Dalton family. It was while in this area, so close to the Sidney-Deadwood Trail, that she began her first serious research at the county courthouse.

But now she was home after giving up her school in the middle of her second year there. The Oliver Hamilton school was vacant, so she signed up for that and went to the Grandma Hunzicker home to board during the week. This was a fun time for her. She had always been reserved around us boys, but now she played the part of a gay divorcee. She had style, dash, and was light on her feet. We were delighted to take her to a dance every Saturday night, even if we had to work all week to overhaul a Model T engine, babbitt the connecting rods, and change the clutch bands. We were happy to do it. She didn't seem to mind our rough manners, and we ignored her divorce.

Even men years younger than she became fascinated as she brushed them off with good grace.

It was March before we could get repairs and fix the threshing machine. Strasburgers cancelled the farm lease because they said the contract was not lived up to; the rye should have been threshed in the fall, which it should have. Ed Strasburger wanted an extra load of rye for compensation, and when we got to the bin, he had it loaded, ready to go. A brother of mine jumped into Ed's wagon and said, "To hell with you," and with his scoop shovel, proceeded to unload the grain into our wagon.

We had been having fabulous luck, and it began to look like we couldn't fail. James boasted he'd be retired in ten years. George Hare even said one time, "The goddam Sandozes are going to take over the whole country." However, he was premature with his prediction. As if Mama's prophecy about the corn had come true, luck turned against us. The depression following World War I came on, muskrat hides became practically worthless, and a drouth settled in. Listed corn rows blew level, cutworms arrived in unbelievable numbers, and the grasshoppers came to destroy everything green. On top of it all, we had lost the trapping.

James began to have a yen to own land, so we sent to the *Denver Post* to answer what was advertised in the *Empire* section. We caught a ride to Alliance and went on the train. The mountains looked so close to the depot that we started walking. After trudging along all day, we were still only in the foothills, so we got on a train going to the west slope of the Rockies, near the Colorado River.

There was no way to use this land; it was so rocky, one could scrape all day and not get a scoopful. There was no trapping because everything was already frozen at that altitude. When James wanted to take a small boat we'd bought and float down the Royal Gorge—he had no idea of the Grand Canyon, he'd never even finished the eighth grade and had never been away from home before—I knew I had to get him out of there, because he was just headstrong enough to try it. Instead, we went up to Big Piney in Wyoming and looked the land situation over. We didn't like what we found, so came back to Alliance on the train. By waiting, we could have caught a ride home on a freight wagon, but we were both homesick, so we bought a round of cheese, a big box of crackers, and started walking. We got about half-way home, stopping at every windmill to eat and drink, before night came. We crawled into a haystack to spend the dark hours. The next day, we got home with blisters on our feet and disappointment with the mountains.

Papa didn't have any faith in banks, and he discouraged us boys from putting our money on deposit where it could have drawn interest. For a couple of years, we had hid it in the chimney stand in our bunkhouse in carbide cans. Then we put it in his safe, only it wasn't so safe. He could not differentiate between his money and ours, and when we found about three hundred dollars missing, we decided we'd better put the rest in land, for sure.

The Modisetts, Albert and Mayre, had been loaning money for years to the settlers and then claiming the land in foreclosure. They amassed a big block in their ranch, but still had many outlying pieces they wanted to sell.

James decided to buy one of their places thirty miles
northeast in Cherry County. There was an old sodhouse
on it, but very little meadow land. However, it gave us
new stomping grounds. I found a collection of girls
down there that I thought I felt more comfortable with
and on hunting trips managed to stop at various places.
But the hound man is not always welcomed, either by the
father who thinks a man's first loyalty will be to his dogs,
nor by the rancher who resents having strangers crossing
his place and possibly making money off him, and surely
not by the girl who can distinctly smell the doggy scent,
as well as the hide smell.

I was over twenty-one now and eligible for a homestead if there were any. Papa found 46 acres right by the
Four-Inch Windmill in the Spade range. There were some
of these isolated unhomesteaded tracts, and most people
thought no one would ever find them in the abstract-
owned property. I filed and built a twelve- by fourteen-
foot house, a shack I used mostly for storing grain. Most
of the ground was level, and I broke it up for corn. A
neighbor had been using the land free, so I made an
enemy right away. Before that, he had been one of my
better friends.

It began to seem that I needed a wife. But this place was
not big enough to make a living on. After our family
bought the Spade land adjoining, I sold it to them. Then I
bought the Van Wagner place, about a section, for a dollar
and a half an acre. It lay about six miles northwest of our
Sandhills orchards, and, while it had a nice valley called
Curlew, the hills were the most worthless in the area. This
place laid just south of the Worena Hill we used as a

staging point in our surveying many years before. Ten years later, if it had not been for the Roosevelt moratorium on mortgage payments, I would have lost it, even at that ridiculously low price.

But now I found that girls want love first and then a place to live. I tried to correlate the two, but found it difficult. I didn't want a Catholic because of our Calvinist background, nor a "doll" that I would have to wait on. Surely not a divorcee.

I bought a homesteader's shack from the top of the hill south of Ransom Hamilton's home in the Hyland Flat. A lone tree still stands up there that promotes a lot of verbal garbage about how it was a local hanging tree for settlers. I loaded the house on a long wagon right beside the spot when the shoot was so little it wouldn't have shaded a gopher pile. That was to be my honeymoon cottage if I could just find someone to share it with me. I knew several nice Catholic girls; I thought maybe I could change their minds about religion, but not much luck. Papa began to be irritated at my spending so much time "girling." I thought maybe I'd impress him with some of the letters I got and pinned them up on the wall. All that came of this was my sisters learned not to put any of their feelings into a letter to a boyfriend.

I had kind of a girl friend up on Box Butte and another in Cherry County some hundred miles apart. I'd go west on Saturday night to a dance in a stripped-down Ford, and I mean stripped down, no fenders or such excess. One morning on my way home, I raced on the right-of-way with Zurchers and upset in the barrow pit. They stopped and helped me right the Ford. The steering wheel had come off. I stuck that back on and went on

down the road waving that removable piece. When I got
home, there were several girls at our place with their
parents. Papa was so mad, he warned those girls that I
was a no-good. So I drove on down thirty miles to the
girl friend in Cherry County. There they had a small
bitch with a litter of pups in the cellar-way. Usually dogs
were my friends, but not this one. She bit me, and I
wound up next day at the doctor's to get a tetanus shot. So
that romantic Sunday had not been such a success.

Some way it seemed easier for me to act natural around
married women, or those that had been married. When a
grass widow, a Mrs. Kline, took our school to teach, I
began frequenting the Dovers, where she boarded. I was
again in competition with Carl Mills, who visited there
also. But I can thank her for telling me quite a bit about
the birds and the bees, even if she wasn't what I called
wife material, having been divorced, and Mama so
against it. But I was always glad for her advice, even if it
still didn't help my popularity.

Chapter XIII

Married at Twenty-eight

With girls so scarce in the country, it was easy for my own sisters to be popular. Flora had several of the neighbor boys coming to the place, ostensibly for gasoline or cigarettes, since Papa took a dim view of her dating. But she could go along with any of us brothers and dance every set. Johnny Myers, the lean and lank cowboy, came every Sunday to see us boys and teach Caroline how to second on the organ, but he really came to see Flora, while some of us danced or just listened to him play the fiddle. We all grew very fond of him.

But then came my second shocking brush with death, a fact that had so upset my life with Grossmutter in those far-off Riverplace days. Johnny had been coming regularly every Sunday since Flora had come home in May. But this Sunday in August he did not come. He was not there for dinner, nor later in the afternoon. Different ones of us wondered out loud about him and watched that east road with every nerve tense. The day passed, but Johnny never came. There were no telephones, and only later on Monday did we hear that he had gotten appendicitis down in Cherry County on the Dille ranch where he worked. There were no doctors for miles, and he had died without medical help. I drove my old Ford down as soon as possible to see what I could do to help. I met his sister Flossie, who had come to accompany the coroner from Hyannis to take charge of the body. On Monday in haying season and hot weather, the coroner could find no one who would help him embalm in his shop back of the hotel. He asked me and, while I'd never done anything of that sort, I didn't feel I could refuse.

There was no money to send the body for burial in Missouri where the family lived since leaving the Sandhills, so I loaned Flossie money enough for two tickets and went sadly home. In spite of our problems with the threshing, we still had been good buddies, and Flossie had been one of my favorite dancing partners.

We were doing less hunting all the time; furs were cheap, and other things seemed to be lessening our interest. We did occasionally go some place to hunt out an obnoxious coyote that was getting into someone's turkeys. This happened at Bixby's, and they sent for us to come and hunt on their ranch some twelve miles southeast. James and I went down, but we didn't find any coyotes that first day, so left the hounds there for a time. Later we went down and hunted again. It came evening and the old maid sister, Ina, made supper and asked us to spend the night. She lived there with her mother and brother, Onie. When it came time to go to bed, Ina went with us upstairs to show us our room. As she went out, she handed us each a couple of garments. "I knew you wouldn't have any night clothes along." We were still not exactly civilized; those were the first pajamas we'd seen, except in the Sears Roebuck catalog.

After our trapping for Margraves in the Heywood, Fritz broke up with Frances Macumber, and she married Sam Piper. Our brother became anxious to change territories and managed to rent a four-thousand-acre sandhole fourteen miles south of Seneca. John Russell, who'd worked for Papa at times, went along with him for moral support, company, and, sometimes, hired help. It was open country from his place to the Dismal River, owned by the Federal Land Bank through foreclosure, and there was little attention paid to who was running livestock on it. It looked like a golden opportunity, except that there was no hay land.

James was spending more and more time in Cherry County, so our family was breaking up. There was no man available now when I wanted to break a horse. Since Caroline was always so anxious to get out of the house, it was easy to get her to help. I'd get a bronc in, get it saddled and bridled in the corral, then work it out into the open. Caroline would ride alongside riding Blackie, but since she rode without a saddle, I couldn't snub my horse to the saddlehorn. She would get her hands on both ears of my horse, twisting to distract the horse. Then, sinking her teeth into one of the ears as she'd seen us do many, many times, she would have the bronc under control long enough for me to grab the headstall in one hand, the saddlehorn in the other, and swing aboard.

Caroline would let go, spitting and gagging, but I was

on and ready. As soon as the bronc felt its ears free, we were off, my horse twisting and turning, rearing and sidestepping, while I pulled leather and hoped the cinch would hold. It wasn't stylish riding, but I had to control and hang on any way I could; it would be too dangerous to get off or be thrown. Soon we would be off running, Caroline riding frantically on one side and then the other, outrunning my horse to keep it out of fences, machinery, and off high hills. She tried to keep me on a flat, going straight. Soon we'd be riding along for a mile or so, until our horses were tired, and mine settled down to less bucking and more trotting. After a couple of these sessions, I was ready for a longer ride, and I'd have to invent someplace to go, preferably with some other riders.

Often it was somewhere like Aults Grove, half-way to the Mirage Flats some twenty miles off, where they had a dance pavilion. These were long rides and often my horse would give out before I got home, and I'd come in carrying my saddle in the grey of dawn.

After I'd moved to the Van Wagner place, if a horse didn't break out well to the saddle, I'd teach it to work in the harness, and those descendants of the wild Fox mare of the Riverplace surely needed that. Sometimes I'd hitch Blackie to a light wagon, and my sister would hold her from the offside, while I brought the bronc around. I'd hook the neckyoke and fasten the tugs while holding the triprope on the new horse. Then I'd get into the wagon with the lines and rope. Ordinarily, another man would hold the rope, but I thought this too dangerous for Caroline and, anyway, she wouldn't be strong enough.

At the first slack in the rope, we were off. The bronc would lunge first, taking the wagon along. But immediately Blackie would jump ahead and outrun her team mate, managing to keep us going in a circle around my valley in the Curlew where there were no fences. After a few rounds over the rough ground—where Lawrence Macumber had plowed the previous year with a round of summer sausage on one plow handle and a jug on the other, missing a furrow here and there—the wagon box jumping ever higher, almost above the bolster, the bronc would be ready to lean into Blackie for comfort. I'd drive back and pick up my sister and go for another few rounds, with her saddlehorse doing most of the pulling. Most of those Fox horses weighed only eight or nine hundred pounds and had little "sand."

I kept busy improving my Van Wagner place, living there and hauling rye to town. Back home, everything was overflowing with grain—the back end of the bunk-house, my homestead house on the Forty, the granary. I built an elongated wagon box of foot boards that held about 75 bushels and hauled it to town for 40 and 45 cents a bushel.

George Hare sold me a team of gray horses, Prince and Nellie. They were Percherons, and rugged. They were not the balky, inbred, dinky horses that Papa had. They had size and substance, and one morning after I'd stayed overnight on the Niobrara, I came to Rush Creek about three miles south of Rushville. The wooden bridge there was without a railing and had an exposed drop-off of some 15 feet on either side into the running creek. It was an icy November day that had started with fog and rain that turned into sleet and glare ice. None of my six horses was shod, not the four abreast, nor the two, Prince and

Nellie, in the lead. As we started the rise, the bridge being
at an angle, I could feel disaster. The horses' hooves were
not holding; the animals were scared of the bridge; and it
was all I could do to keep myself upright, braced against
the front endgate as the horses leaned into their harnesses.
About halfway across, the wagon began to slide sideways on the wide iron tires, and it seemed there was
nothing to hold us. I leaned as high as I could, hollered
out wildly as I could, "Prince, you son-of-a-bitch; Nellie,
git in there." That was language they understood. Together, that lead team with their front feet now off the
bridge and on solid ground, they alone dragged that
wagon back from the brink, the four wheel horses slip-
ping and sliding to keep up. The 70 bushels of rye was still
intact, and maybe even my life saved. Halfway up the
hill, but off the bridge, I jumped off, grabbed a couple of
rocks to stick under the wheels, and let the horses rest.
Tying the lines, I went up front, lifted the leather collars
first from Nellie and then from Prince, and wiped away
the sweat with my red handkerchief. I'd never even
hoped to own horses like that!

But our most dependable outlet for grain after Prohibition was to bootleggers. The Sandhills were full of them,
because the sheriff and the townspeople hesitated to go
out on those sandy trails with the hard tires we had then.
Sheriff Bruce did come down once to find seven barrels of
mash in the Big Hill blowouts. He dumped the mash and
took Frank Wildman, our local New Yorker from the
tough Lower East Side, to jail, but nothing happened.
Frank knew how to contend with much tougher law than
Sheriff Bruce could muster. But we were never tempted

to bootleg ourselves. Papa caused a furor enough in the family by patronizing bootleggers for his evening hot toddy.

The years got drier, and I tried to hold up the water level in my Curlew Valley by putting down more wells. These were sand-bucketed affairs forty or fifty feet deep under a wooden tower run by cobbled-up pieces of various old Spade mills that had lain for a generation in a sandhole someplace. I even invented one made of two fifteen-gallon drums, cut in half to catch the breeze. I finally had seven makeshift wells on the eighty acres of valley, but they only created small waterholes against the drouth years that were already coming.

I was no longer on the good farm land of the Macumber place, nor did I even have hounds. Without the dried muskrat meat, they could neither run nor fight. I knew if I could just get hold of some good swamp land, I could have hounds again, and spending money. But the times would have to change a lot before any really good land would come on the market. It was all in the hands of big ranchers. And yet my eyes always came back to that certain long, green valley dotted with springs and willow trees, with muskrat houses in winter. It had the first spring holes some fifteen miles east of Pine Creek across a kind of hump in the Sandhills. This was the first valley with permanent water on the east side of the Cambrian arch that underlies this part of the Panhandle of Nebraska. But it would take a drastic financial crisis to make it available.

One Saturday in the spring of 1923, Caroline and I were getting ready to go to a dance at the Strasburger schoolhouse over southwest. She was not allowed to date, but could go with me. About noon, Frank and William Kicken came up to visit from their home about halfway to Lakeside. They were accompanied by a young lady I'd not seen for ten years or more, a daughter of William. She had been living in Denver, going to high school. Now the family had come to live with his brother Frank near their homestead where I'd herded cattle years before. Papa suggested that we take Mary along. She had a bit of the city about her, even to the pinkish-red stockings she wore. Our friend Boris Kicken was her cousin, and I was proud to have this lady for my partner, for we soon forgot Caroline and became a couple. The dance was lots of fun, and I enjoyed showing off a new girl. Caroline went to sleep on the way home, and we visited about many things.

We had a great deal in common, and the next Saturday, I went down to the Kickens' without my sister. I no longer needed her along for a foil. I'd finally found what I thought I was looking for, and, of course, Papa was happy that I'd found a fine French woman among his friends.

The next spring, in February, we were married, which ends this part of my story. It brought me into a whole new way of life, and eventually we were able to move into my beloved Willow Valley. But that is for another whole book for someone else to write.